December 1992

THE
BIG SANDY VALLEY

BOOKS BY

WILLARD ROUSE JILLSON

GEOLOGY

Oil and Gas Resources of Kentucky, 1919-1920
Geology and Coals of Stinking Creek, 1919
Contributions to Kentucky Geology, 1920
Economic Papers on Kentucky Geology, 1921
Production of Eastern Kentucky Crude Oils, 1921
The Sixth Geological Survey, 1921
Oil Field Stratigraphy of Kentucky, 1922
Conservation of Natural Gas in Kentucky, 1922
Geological Research in Kentucky, 1923
The Coal Industry in Kentucky, 1922-1924
Kentucky State Parks, 1924
Mineral Resources of Kentucky, 1926
New Oil Pools of Kentucky, 1926
Mineral Resources of Louisville, 1926
Topography of Kentucky, 1927

HISTORY

The Big Sandy Valley, 1923
The Kentucky Land Grants, 1925
Old Kentucky Entries and Deeds, 1926

BIOGRAPHY

Edwin P Morrow—Kentuckian, 1922

VERSE

Songs and Satires, 1920

THE BEAUTIFUL BIG SANDY

This view on the Levisa Fork a few miles above Prestonsburg in Floyd County shows the river and the valley as it appeared during the period of settlement.

THE
BIG SANDY VALLEY

A Regional History Prior
to the Year 1850

BY

WILLARD ROUSE JILLSON, Sc. D.

State Geologist of Kentucky

Member of the
American Historical Association
Kentucky State Historical Society
The Filson Club

Boone Day Address, 1922
Kentucky State Historical Society

WITH A NEW FOREWORD
by
WILLARD ROUSE JILLSON

Baltimore

REGIONAL PUBLISHING COMPANY

1970

Originally Published
Louisville, 1923

Reprinted with permission and a new Foreword
Regional Publishing Company
Baltimore, 1970

International Standard Book Number 0-8063-7981-2
Library of Congress Catalog Card Number 70-85503

The publisher gratefully acknowledges
the loan of the original of this book
by the
Cox Library
Tucson, Arizona

Made in the United States of America

Dedicated to

BIG SANDIANS

Everywhere

CONTENTS

ILLUSTRATIONS

Foreword to the Second Edition

Coming to Eastern Kentucky from central-northern Oklahoma in the late Spring of 1917, the author of this history was fortunate in making within a year or so the lasting acquaintance of a number of reputable, elderly men and women who were quite generally recognized to be direct third or fourth generation descendants of some of the leading land-owning pioneers of this rugged part of the State. Somewhat later, during the Autumn of 1922 on down into the early Spring of 1923, when the manuscript pages of this book on the early history of the Big Sandy Valley were being completed, the principal incidents of not a few tales told to me by one or more of these genial "old timers" served very timely and well to fill in and make more complete this narrative of the exploration and settlement of the mountain and valley province of the easternmost part of the State.

Nearly 300 years have passed since two intrepid explorers of English ancestry, James Needham and Gabriel Arthur, coursing their way down the placid Ohio River, passed the debouchure of the Big Sandy on their way to the Tennessee River which they ascended to its headwaters on their way back to the Eastern Seaboard. Somewhat later, if many a variant tale may be depended upon, came the fabulous John Swift, and after him, Daniel Boone and many another of lesser fame to explore for a while and then return to the Settlements away to the East. Toward the close of the Seventeenth Century, in the year 1784 to be exact, John Graham, a well educated and opulent native of Virginia, gifted and experienced as a land surveyor appeared in Kentucky and began surveying and taking up in a strictly legal manner vast stretches of wild land. Although his first surveys were laid down on lands closely bordering on the east the far-famed Bluegrass Country, his largest group of surveys—some 110 or more, involving a calculated 366,771 acres were located in what was at that time—1808 to 1819—Floyd County in the upper Big Sandy Valley.

As his land acquiring exploits continued down through the years from the first surveys and purchases in Mason County in 1797 to the last Floyd County acquisitions by Land Warrant in the year 1832, John Graham became by wide and large, one in truth might say, the outstanding man and the richest individual in the Big Sandy Valley—a Judge of Floyd County, an individual banker in Prestonsburg and a member of the Kentucky Legislature seated at Frankfort. In the latter years of his life more than 375,000 acres of land passed through his hands, a single fact which gives some dependable measure of his importance in the hill and vale country of Eastern Kentucky. Within the pages of this book, besides the highlights of the unusual career of Judge Graham, there will be found by the close and careful reader, many interesting biographical references to other outstanding early residents of the Big Sandy whose names and deeds, except for their portrayal here, would be entirely lost to posterity.

Because of this fact, the astute men of long vision of Maryland who have set their hands and hearts to the second printing of this book have brought new and added light to a clear and faithful picture of "Early Times up Big Sandy" hardly to be found elsewhere in any library, book-stall or private historical collection. For this service to early American history of the Mid-West, they deserve not only the unmeasured thanks and approval of today, but for all the time to come that our beloved country may endure. With these few remarks the writer in unaffected sincerity, lays aside this rambling postscript with the age old remark and truism, *finis ecce laborum!*

W. R. JILLSON

Frankfort, Kentucky.
February 23, 1970.

PREFACE

WHILE there are several very good general histories of Kentucky, the number of regional histories is small indeed. Several of the general Kentucky histories are in effect little more than histories of the Bluegrass and Ohio River country held together by a slender thread of centralized political adventure. None of the Kentucky histories treat of the "mountain" or eastern portion of Kentucky adequately. Some of them scarcely mention it.

No real history of the Big Sandy has ever been written, although one or two biographical sketch books loosely bound together by a train of inaccurate historical generalities have been presented. In the preparation of this work a great many sources have been examined, including those listed in the attached bibliography. These latter titles were reviewed in considerable detail, and in some few instances lightly excerpted. The principal part of the subject matter of these pages was given as the "Boone Day" address, June 7, 1922, before the Kentucky State Historical Society, in Frankfort, Ky. This was later published in the September, 1922, number of the "Register," since when it has been completely revised and greatly expanded.

It will be noted that this history covers the geological, prehistorical and pioneering period of the Big Sandy Valley. The account ends with the year 1850. It is essentially, therefore, a "log cabin history" of this portion of eastern Kentucky. A serious attempt has been made in the choice of the subject matter and illustrations to avoid references or comparison to the Big Sandy Valley of to-day, an accurate account of which would form so vivid a contrast with that contained within these covers.

Critics may point out that this history lacks much in the way of local and personal tradition and incident. This is indeed true. Biographical material—available at every hand—has been purposely withheld. Volumes of this character, exhaling a somewhat mercenary flavor, are met with all too frequently. The attempt has been made to hold to the truth as it was found, thus producing a book documentarily correct rather than traditionally so.

As these last pages go to the publisher, the writer feels, with deep sincerity, that only a part of the story of the early days in the Big Sandy Valley has been told. A lifetime, instead of a few short busy years, might well have been spent in collecting the data that could be made available. If, with its many imperfections, a thoughtful perusal of this little book shall give a faithful picture of the heroic past in the Big Sandy Valley, and at the same time inspire the writing of a fuller and up-to-date account of the region, it will have served its purpose well.

Frankfort, Kentucky.
March 15, 1923.

THE
BIG SANDY VALLEY

CHAPTER I

THE WILDERNESS

Last of the great natural provinces of Kentucky to be wrested by the pioneer from the savage Shawnee and Cherokee, the Big Sandy Valley region is literally an unexplored treasure-trove of documentary history and romantic tradition. Out of the age-old darkness and mystery of an unpeopled wilderness, down through the dawn of prehistoric times to the days of our grandfathers, runs the continuous thread of a story of stirring adventure and noble sacrifice. In the flight of the unnumbered years the occasional and indistinct forest trail became a well-defined path, and then a public road. Canebrake and natural meadow gave way before the advancing fields of golden corn, and idle mountain streams lilting along from their craggy sources came to take up their burden of industry at many an improvised splash dam and old log mill. The subdued, half-hidden smudge of the dusky savage, faintly painted against the forest wall, became in time the welcoming hearth fire of the hardy homesteader. Herds of cattle and sheep replaced the wild, nomadic buffalo, and close to the confluence of

the larger streams, outlying stations and rude
log forts, hastily raised by the hands of daring
scouts, grew into settlements and towns with a
thriving industry based upon the rich forest,
agricultural, and mineral wealth of the region.
At last the painted aborigine departed; his
favorite hunting ground usurped and turned to
nobler ends, there came to stand in his heritage
a conquering race of almost pure Anglo-Saxon
blood which, as the years have passed, has
concerned itself, not so much with the heroic
deeds of its fathers as with the absorbing
problems of an extended civilization, conscious
of its growing importance in the social and
economic fabric of the Commonwealth.

GEOLOGIC HISTORY

Situated in the easternmost part of Kentucky, the Big Sandy Valley is an integral part
of the Southern Appalachians. It reaches
northward from the Cumberland Mountains
on the southeast through a broad, maturely
dissected region known as the Cumberland
Plateau to the low lands along the Ohio
River. The valley of the Big Sandy, including those parts which lie in Virginia and
West Virginia, comprises an area of 4,182
square miles. It is a unit within the Southern

Appalachian coal field, its rocks being composed of sandstones, shales, coals, and a few thin limestones, all of Pennsylvanian age. These sediments are referable in ascending order to the Pottsville, Conemaugh and Allegheny formations, or the productive Coal Measures.

A single outcrop of limited extent which takes exception to the above statement, is found on the north flank of Pine Mountain, in Pike and Letcher, from the "Breaks of Sandy" to "Pound Gap," where limestones, sandstones, and shales of the Mississippian and Devonian age have been exposed by the Pine Mountain thrust fault. These formations are not coal bearing. The surface rocks in the Big Sandy region are composed of sediments deposited in shallow water. The occurrence of the numerous coal seams indicates that in the far off Coal Measure time this area was one which bordered closely upon a brackish water embayment, perhaps of the lagoon type. For countless ages, Pennsylvanian sediments continued to be deposited in this region until they reached, in the southeast, the enormous thickness of 3,000 to 5,000 feet.

As the Pennsylvanian (Coal Measure) period drew to a close through crustal movements initiated by the oncoming Appalachian

Revolution, emergence took place in the upper Big Sandy Valley and some contiguous regions. The uplift marked the birth struggles of a broad interior continental area which was later to enclose all of Kentucky. The new land lay about 100 miles to the southeast of the old Cincinnati Island—the Bluegrass region of central Kentucky which had existed in insular figure at various intervals from the Middle Ordovician (Trenton) period. Emergence and erosion, depression and sedimentation in cyclic sequence with a positive uplift throughout the latter part of the Paleozoic era, had given it a well defined physical relief with which to face the emergent Coal Measures of the Southeast.

Coincident with the uplift of the region now occupied by the upper Big Sandy, erosion began, the waters flowing generally to the north and northwest over a widening plain. The highest points or headwaters at this early time were undoubtedly within the western portions of the States of Virginia, North Carolina, and eastern Tennessee. Topographically the headwaters region of the Big Sandy River, as we know it to-day, was then a part of a broad lowland backed by a sinking hill and mountain country to the southeast, known as the "Lost Appalachia," a large elongated continental body of Paleozoic times, the central axis of which was about coincident with the Piedmont belt, and extended to a distant, though undefined eastern boundary in the Atlantic. Its known northern limits were in Newfoundland, while by the way of Florida and the West Indies it connected with South America.

The rising interior lowland faced a great shallow inland sea on the northwest. An arm of this sea occupied a portion of Kentucky, and covered in particular that region which is known as the western border of the Eastern Coal Field. Shore marshes, inland swamps, and a few small lakes occupying slight depressions formed during Coal Measure time were characteristic figures of the landscape. All of the newly exposed strata were soft and unconsolidated. Nowhere in the Big Sandy Valley, then taking form, were there any high elevations. The boundaries of all drainage areas were poorly defined. A vegetation closely resembling that of the Coal Measures covered the lowlands, but the highlands to the southeast were probably more or less barren, due to low temperatures, an inconstant moisture, and thin soil.

Along the Kentucky-Virginia line the Pine Mountain was slowly taking anticlinal figure, but in the soft surface sediments of that period its structural outline was at first but slightly reflected in the topography if at all. The major drainage crossed this embryo mountain of elevation at the "Breaks of Sandy" and at the Pound Gap without difficulty. Minor streams also undoubtedly crossed it at many a point long since effaced by the tireless hand of erosion. Ages passed. The Pine Mountain fold grew in figure as pressures exerted by the mountain-making forces in the southeast continued. Finally it became an overturned anticline and then by two distinct movements was thrust faulted to the northwest a total distance of several miles. In the course of these great dynamics, the great Russell Fork fault, to which the river by that name in Dickenson and Buchanan Counties, Virginia, became consequent, was developed. As these crustal changes approached completion, a new drainage pattern in the western headwaters of the Big Sandy slowly adjusted itself. A score or more of streams which had originally crossed the Pine Mountain region and had been beheaded during that great uplift were turned back upon themselves or otherwise diverted to form Elkhorn Creek and the Pound River.

Up to this time the Tug and Levisa Forks were undoubtedly separate streams emptying into the elongated Northeast-Southwest upper Pennsylvanian embayment of eastern Kentucky. At first little more than creeks they gradually extended their lower courses to the northwest as the Appalachian uplift continued. In due course, as the semi-marine waters receded, these streams grew to be rivers of large figure. The Levisa Fork of the Big Sandy River extended its lower course to the northwest until it encountered the Paint Creek Uplift then in progress of emergence in Johnson, Morgan, Magoffin, Lawrence, and Floyd Counties. This relatively small structural feature occupied at the time an insular and strategic position. It exhibited an independent and somewhat radial drainage.

In due course the Paint Creek Uplift contributed a part of its drainage to the Levisa Fork, and shunted the major stream to the northeast. The result was the juncture of the Levisa and Tug Forks and the formation during the early Permian of the infant Big Sandy River. The period was unique. The entire State stood for the first time in all geological history a unit land area. River systems were taking figure everywhere. The new major stream of far eastern Kentucky was similar in its geographic character to the Big Sandy of to-day, but because of its youth it lacked the present closely meandering and deeply intrenched characteristic, except at the "Breaks of Sandy." At this point the present thousand-foot gorge was in progress of formation with the recession of the ancient Russell Fork Falls, which was probably one or two hundred feet high when it broke over the uplifted Pottsville conglomerates of Pine Mountain.

In the course of Mesozoic time the original headwaters of the Big Sandy were gradually reduced in area by the transverse piratical advances of the headwaters of the Clinch and Blue Stone rivers. These streams extended their main headwaters along favorable structural lines which were developed during the early period of Appalachian Mountain making. Compensating itself for these remote headwaters losses, the Big Sandy at the same time, and later well through the Cenozoic era, played thief with the drainage of some of its neighbors in both its upper and lower courses. The headwaters of the North Fork of the Kentucky River south of Pine Mountain were diverted to the Pound Fork of the Big Sandy during the folding which resulted in the elevation of this great mountain range. The Pound Gap was left as a record of the modification. Further

THE "BREAKS OF SANDY"

Where the Russell Fork of the Big Sandy River crosses the Pine Mountain—the Kentucky-Virginia State line—it has cut a gorge in the Pottsville conglomeratic sandstones 1,000 feet deep.

down, the Levisa Fork near Prestonsburg extended the upper waters of Right Middle Creek, thus effecting the capture of a part of the Burning Fork of the Licking. As a result creek waters which originally flowed to the northwest were reversed to the southeast. One of the most notable of these several piracies is that of upper Paint Creek—the old Elk Fork of the Licking River. In effecting this gigantic piracy the Levisa Fork added not less than 100 square miles to the drainage area of the Big Sandy River.

Had it not been for the occurrence of the extraordinary uplift in the Paint Creek region during these early Post-Pottsville times, the Levisa River would most certainly have been the principal headwaters fork of the Licking. The Big Sandy, greatly reduced in size, would have been confined to the Tug Fork and its tributaries. These geological facts are worthy of serious consideration, for the early deflection of this stream from its intended course has had a permanent effect on eastern Kentucky. If the Levisa River had not been thwarted in its attempt to join the Licking, waters now passing through the "Breaks of Sandy" would have first mingled with those of the Ohio at Cincinnati. A high barrier ridge would have

effectively separated Paintsville and all up-
river points from Louisa, and the Ohio at
Catlettsburg and Ashland; and all subsequent
history for this broad region of eastern Kentucky would have been vastly different from
that which has been recorded.

As the regional uplift continued, and the
drainage of the Big Sandy River and its
tributaries perfected itself, the first soft sediments were worn away, leaving the harder
underlying rocks exposed. At the same time a
flora transitional between that of the Coal
Measure period and that which we know to-day
came to take its place over the newly carved low
hills and broad valleys. Through the succession
of the ages, while a well rounded cycle of slowly
changing climates perpetuated itself, hundreds,
perhaps thousands, of feet of loose and semi-
consolidated sediments were removed by the
streams tributary to the Big Sandy River. As
Mesozoic time sped on, the mother river and its
numerous progeny of creeks and branches
became old. The intervening hills and plateaus
which were born of the Post-Paleozoic uplift
gradually melted away. The Pine Mountain,
the only ridge of structural elevation in the
Valley, alone remained following this long
beveling process as an outstanding topographic
feature.

A broadly meandering habit slowly fixed itself on the Big Sandy and its larger creeks, presaging the advent of the Cretaceous period and regional peneplaination. Shortly following the beginning of Cenozoic time widespread uplift again took place. This resulted in the rejuvenation of the entire Big Sandy drainage system and brought about the entrenchment of the streams in their now well defined meanders. During this vast lapse of time, an old and grotesque group of reptiles and amphibia arose, occupied and dominated the land, and then departed. Coincident with their decline, came the first birds, the early mammals, and the ancestral broad-leafed plants and trees.

Gradually, as the innumerable seasons came and went, the figure of the hills and the streams became much the same as it is to-day. Then there was ushered in the last great cold period, which brought down high walls of glacier ice into the Ohio Valley. With it, for a time at least, an arctic fauna and flora came to possess the Big Sandy Valley, as it did all of eastern Kentucky. In the fiord-like waters of the lower Big Sandy icebergs broken from this great continental glacier carrying igneous pebbles of Canadian origin floated many miles south of

Louisa before they melted and disappeared. When later, in the course of time, the ice finally disappeared, the various species of animals and plants known to us to-day, and others not distantly related, gradually migrated and took possession of the land. In the interim between the first uplift of this region and the present there had passed away the entire Mesozoic and Cenozoic eras, a lapse of time so great as to preclude accurate determination, but probably not less than fifty million years, and possibly much longer. During all this time the Big Sandy Valley had been a land area.

Prehistoric Man

With the retreat of glaciation, there was ushered in the latter part of the Pleistocene period, during which an equitable climate brought into the Big Sandy Valley a flora and fauna which, with the exception of domesticated animals and man, has been designated as native. Who can adequately describe the awe-inspiring silences of this great hill and mountain region into which no human foot had as yet penetrated? Nature played her hand in the open. Forest animals, except for their natural enemies, felt no fear, and throughout the countless days and nights, as became their habit, sought out their food and their mates, unconscious of coming disaster in the slow but certain migration eastward across the North American continent of the nomadic aborigine.

At length in the fulfillment of the years man came, not as a queer, contorted, grotesque race of low humans, but as a rather high paleolithic ancestor of the Indian which we know as of yesterday. The first inhabitants of the Big Sandy Valley, like those of the central portion of the State to whom they were closely related, were sturdy, copper-colored tribesmen, possibly the ancestors of the Cherokee Indians.[1] These "Mound Builders," as they have come to be called, were essentially an agricultural people, dependent upon the soil for their chief food supply. They probably made their first entrance into Kentucky and the Big Sandy Valley about two thousand years ago. That they were largely agricultural is indicated by their remains which, in the form of mounds, tumuli and other earth works used for burying grounds, fortifications, and ceremonial purposes,[2] are always found in the region of good soil. There was, however, no great difference in the game found in such regions and that of the more sterile or rocky sections.

Of the many mounds that have been found in the Big Sandy Valley, the five discovered above the mouth of Paint Creek in the Big Sandy bottom are probably the most important. Excavations made in some of these during recent years have shown skeletons, arrowheads, stone axes, charcoal, and other paleolithic remains.[3] Farther down on the Big Sandy about its mouth, and in the Ohio River bottoms adjacent, there have been located from time to time a number of mounds from which have been taken several skeletons and many crude native utensils. The same region has also been so prolific in its production of human skeleton material as to indicate that it may have been a prehistoric battle-ground.[4]

With the advent of the buffalo into the eastern United States and Kentucky about the year 1000 A. D., a great change came over the Mound Builder. The necessity of tilling the soil to secure his living became less and less important. The prolific development of the buffalo, the ease with which it was captured, and the bounteous supply of food it provided, turned the thoughts of the industrious ancestral Plains Indian from agricultural pursuits to those of the chase. The inherent blood-loving characteristic of the savage came to dominate him, as the practice of stalking and killing game for food developed. In the end there came to exist a group of warlike tribes in the eastern United States, which gradually forced its way into each agricultural recess occupied by the peace-loving Mound Builder, and finally exterminated him.

ADVENT OF THE INDIAN

With the passing of the Mound Builders, permanent human occupation of the Big Sandy Valley ceased for several hundred years. When the first explorers came, they found this region crossed by many a well defined trail, the favorite hunting-ground of strong and constantly warring Indian tribes, chief among which were the Shawnees and Cherokees. Later the Mingos and Delawares also joined their neighbors and came into this territory.

The Indians knew the Big Sandy River as the Totera, or Toteras, or Toteroy, as some of the Totero tribe had dwelt on it for a time. This tribe was also called the Shattaras. Sometimes the Indians pronounced the name so that it came to be Tateroy, Chateroi, or Chatarrawha. The name signified "river of sand bars."[5] It was known officially in New York and Canada as early as 1699 as the Big

Sandy River of Virginia.[6] Hence in time, even though Dr. Thomas Walker, when he discovered it shortly after June 6, 1750, called it the Louisa River,[7] it became known as the Big Sandy River. The early maps name the river variously. The Nuremburg Map of 1756 names it "Gt. Sandy." Evans in 1755 marked it "Tottery or Big Sandy C." Later in 1776 Pownall on his map of North America called it the "Totteroy" River which, of course, meant "Big Sandy." But those tribes living at more remote points had quite a different name for the Big Sandy. The Miamis called it the "Wepepocone-cepewe,"[8] and the Delawares knew it as the "Sikea-cepe," meaning Salt Creek. The Shawnees knew the river by two names, "Mich-e-cho-be-ka-sepe," meaning the Mystery River; and "Me-tho-to-sepe," or the River of Many Buffalo. Of these two the first is the older name. The Wyandot Indians called the Big Sandy "Sees-ta-ye-an-da-wa," the Fire River, from the natural gas springs which burned along its course.[9]

The various tribes which made use of the Big Sandy Valley as a hunting-ground about the time of the first explorations by Englishmen had their villages to the north, principally in the State of Ohio, and to the south in the

State of Tennessee. In their many excursions through the valley their hunting and scalping parties learned the best routes of travel, the lowest passes, and the most suitable fords. As a rule, they stayed away from the larger waters of the Tug and Levisa forks, choosing the rough, stony ridges and steep slopes in preference to the river bottoms, where frequent crossings were necessary, difficult, and dangerous. Their choice generally lay in the shallow creeks, where tracking was next to impossible, and the gradient low and easy. One principal trail passed down the ridges and small waters of the Tug Fork, and another down the headwaters of the Levisa Fork. Each of these main Big Sandy trails led through one of three passes into the headwaters of the Clinch River Valley. These were the gaps at the heads of the Levisa Fork, the Dry Fork, and the Tug River.[10] It is worth while to note that the main Indian trails of the Big Sandy Valley always crossed the higher mountain ridges at the lowest passes. Frequently they built in these gaps monuments of considerable height to scare away evil spirits, which they regarded as always present.

The highest and most important gap or ''pass'' wholly within the Big Sandy Valley,

known now as the "Pound Gap,"[11] but formerly
as the "Sounding Gap," was frequently used
by the Indians, and is richly associated with
their lore and traditions. The "Breaks of
Sandy," where the Russell Fork courses
through the arched and faulted Pine Mountain
and crosses the Virginia-Kentucky State line,
was regarded with reverence and awe by the
Shawnees and other tribes. It is the most strik-
ing water gap in the Big Sandy Valley, and its
outstanding physical characteristic—a wild and
rugged sandstone gorge 1,000 feet deep in many
places—appealed strongly to the Indian's sense
of the supernatural. The fact that the Pine
Mountain was a great broken or faulted fold
on the earth's crust, showing in outcrop on its
northern flank Pennsylvanian and Mississippian sandstones, limestones, and shales which
should normally have been thousands of feet
below the surface of this region, was, of course,
unknown to him. Yet the hollow sound which
attends the tapping of many of the faulted, and
hence suspended, ledges all along Pine Mountain, and particularly in the "Pound Gap," was
clearly observed. It was his observation of this
fact which resulted in the naming of this important gap as the "Sound Gap," "Pound
Gap" being a corruption of this earlier title.

"THE CUMBERLAND PLATEAU"

From the top of the Pine Mountain at a point near Shelby Gap an excellent view may be secured of the rugged hilltops of the upper Big Sandy Valley.

The occurrence of caves, many of which within the tilted Mississippian strata are small and labyrinthine, was also noted by the aborigine. The Shawnees have a tradition describing a great cave in the base of the Pine Mountain, near the "Breaks of Sandy," which is said to have extended over several miles, and from one side to the other.[12] During a great battle with the Cherokees and other tribes they claimed to have sequestered their women and children in this cave, but the exact location of it is not known, if indeed a cave of such size exists at all. Making due allowance for the enlargement of fancy over fact in tradition, there are many excellent geologic reasons for believing that no cave could possibly extend from the base of one side of the Pine Mountain to the other. Caves large enough to allow the entrance of a number of individual men undoubtedly exist, however, in this region, as do a large number of semi-closed "rockhouses" in the sandstone and limestone cliffs on the face of the mountain. Almost due south of Blue Head Knob on the north flank of the Pine Mountain at an altitude of about 2,250 feet there is a cave of considerable proportions which has been only partly explored. Another with the pit-like characteristics of

great depth is to be found near the Pound Gap.
It is known as the "Lost Cave." But neither
of these caves, though undoubtedly known to
the savage, meet his legendary description of
the great cave at the "Breaks of Sandy."

Although the Indians used the Big Sandy
Valley as a hunting-ground, they frequently
came into the region and situated themselves in
more or less permanent camps for varying
periods while engaged in their hunting and
warring expeditions. The Shawnee warpath
led up out of the Little Sandy Valley across the
southwestern portion of Lawrence County into
Johnson County over Mud Lick Creek. At the
confluence of Little Mud Lick and Big Mud
Lick, north of main Paint Creek, the Shawnees
had an old village. Here in the bottomlands
many Indian implements have been found. At
an early day there were painted at this place
on the clifted sandstones of the creek gorge
a number of odd figures of buffalo and deer
done in red and black colors. Various other
undecipherable hieroglyphics also accompanied
the drawings. All evidences of these primitive
mural decorations have become entirely obliter-
ated through natural weathering processes in
the course of the last twenty-five or thirty
years.[13]

In the vicinity of main Paint Creek early settlers found many of the large trees skinned of their bark with drawings of birds and animals done in red and black on the smooth undertrunk of the tree. About the lower waters of Paint Creek, situated generally on the higher hills, have been found a number of Indian graves.[14] A little farther down the Levisa Fork, about seven or eight miles above the juncture with the Tug River, there existed in early times an old Indian town on a small creek which entered the Big Sandy River from the west.[15] These may have been in part at least the remains of the Totera or Shattera villages or burial places. With the cunning and understanding of woodcraft possessed by his race, the Indian generally located his camps in the Big Sandy near the natural salt licks, where the buffalo, deer, and other animals might be easily stalked. This was the case on Mud Lick Creek, where an old salt lick, which gave the creek its name, existed a short distance above the old encampment. Other salt licks known and frequented by the Indians were found along the Big Sandy from its forks to the Ohio River, on the Tug Fork near Warfield, on Middle Creek, and on Beaver Creek.

NOTES TO CHAPTER I

[1] History of Pioneer Kentucky. Cotterill, p. 38.

[2] Kentucky, A Pioneer Commonwealth. Shaler, p. 46.

[3] The Founding of Harman's Station. Connelley, pp. 54-55.

[4] The Big Sandy Valley. Ely, pp. 458-459.

[5] First Report, Department of Archives and History of West Virginia, Vol. I, p. 252.

[6] History of Kentucky. Kerr, Vol. I, p. 9.

[7] First Explorations of Kentucky (Walker's Journal). Johnston, pp. 67 and 70.

[8] The Wilderness Road. Speed, pp. 71-72.

[9] History of Kentucky. Kerr, Vol. 1, p. 12.

[10] History of Southwest Virginia. Summers, p. 28. Also The Kentucky Mountains. Verhoeff, pp. 67 and 70. Also History of Tazewell County and Southwest Virginia. Pendleton, pp. 269, 273, 277.

[11] Altitude, 2,407 feet above sea level, Pound Quadrangle, U. S. G. S. Topog. Atlas.

[12] History of Kentucky. Kerr, pp. 128-129.

[13] Founding of Harman's Station. Connelley, pp. 50-54.

[14] Founding of Harman's Station. Connelley, pp. 54-55.

[15] Kentucky Land Grant Book 16, p. 465. Land Office, Frankfort, Ky.

CHAPTER II

FIRST EXPLORATIONS

(1674-1775)

The latter part of the seventeenth century witnessed a notable movement of western interior exploration in North America. As early as 1669, the great LaSalle with a few intrepid followers had left the security of the old French settlements of Montreal and Quebec on the St. Lawrence, and had plunged into the then unknown and savage-infested wilderness of central and western New York, and the region about the Great Lakes.[1] LaSalle's hope was a short route to China. A few years later, in 1673, began that notable voyage of discovery which gave to the wondering world the first definite knowledge of the broad, fertile Mississippi Valley, and built an enduring fame for Father James Marquette and his companion, Louis Joliet.

About the same time Englishmen from the old Crown colony of Virginia under the patronage of Colonel Abraham Wood, whose frontier fort stood at tidewater on the James River, were toiling through the Appalachian and Blue

Ridge mountains, also in search of a short trading route to the west. In the year 1671, Captain Thomas Batts and Robert Fallam had pushed their way over the great Appalachian divide and had discovered the middle waters of the Kanawha River in West Virginia.[2] They returned to the East flushed with their notable success, and Colonel Wood, sensing the possibilities of a companion tour of exploration, directed in a more southwesterly direction, sent out in 1673[3] James Needham and Gabriel Arthur, who made their way through to the headwaters of the Tennessee River.

Those who are familiar with the geography of the region under discussion, will see at once that the Big Sandy Valley was thus early circumscribed, but not penetrated, by white men. This situation persisted for many, many years. The physiographic configuration of the Southern Appalachians and its principal drainage which directed early explorations down the Kanawha, Ohio, and Tennessee River valleys, placed a bar before the exploration, settlement and development of the Big Sandy Valley as compared to those regions which adjoin it. For many years after the regions about it were settled, it continued to be an Indian hunting-ground and a place of savage despoliation.

ARTHUR DISCOVERS KENTUCKY

It is notable that an accident resulted in the discovery of the Big Sandy Valley and Kentucky. Had this not happened, it is altogether probable that white men would not have set foot in this easternmost part of Kentucky until much later. In the late winter or early spring of 1674, Gabriel Arthur (who had remained with the Cherokees on the headwaters of the Tennessee as a hostage, following the death of James Needham at the hands of the Ocaneechee) took part in the warring expedition with a band of Cherokees directed against the Shawnee villages located on either side of the Ohio River at the mouth of the Scioto in the vicinity of the present site of Portsmouth. Passing over the headwaters of the Tennessee and down the New River, this band of warriors paid a visit to a related tribe of Moneton Indians on the main waters of the Kanawha. Following their friendly festivities they went three days out of their way to the west to take a "clap" at their ancient enemy, the Shawnee. To do this, they passed along the south shore of the Ohio, and crossed the Big Sandy River near its mouth, in order to gain a southern approach to the Shawnee village.

In accompanying these Cherokees, Gabriel Arthur unconsciously became the first white man to set foot in the Big Sandy Valley and Kentucky. Although it is true that his discovery and adventure in Kentucky did not result in opening up the country to the English colonists at once, there can be no doubt but that through Colonel Wood he contributed much information to residents of seaboard Virginia concerning "the back country." The story of his captivity by the Shawnees and his ultimate return to the Cherokees over a path which was either the Big Sandy or, what is more likely, the "Warriors' Trail," is a story of early exploratory hardship and adventure that has been rarely equaled.[4]

Three-quarters of a century later, in 1742, when western Kentucky and southern Ohio had become well known to the French through the explorations of Father Hennepin, LaSalle and Captain Tonti, a Virginia settler, John Peter Salley, journeyed by boat down the Kanawha, Ohio, and Mississippi Rivers.[5] He was accompanied by John Howard and his son, Josiah Howard, who came as explorers from the East. They represented themselves to Salley as carrying a commission from the Governor to travel westward as far as the Mississippi, and to explore the country. They were to receive a large grant of land for this discovery. It was arranged that an equal share was to be given to each of the men who made the expedition. In passing down the Ohio they were the first white men to see from a boat the mouth of the Big Sandy, which at that time was an unexplored wilderness. Half a century later the route they had taken, but did not mark, became the great inland water highway of westward immigration. Salley and his party made their journey to New Orleans, experiencing no trouble with the Indians in the Ohio Valley, who at this time had not yet become extremely hostile to the English. On the Mississippi River the little party was captured by the French and sent to New Orleans, where they were afterward released.

Work of Walker and Gist

Probably the most notable of the early explorers of the Big Sandy Valley was Dr. Thomas Walker, who with his party, after entering Kentucky through Cumberland Gap, proceeded in a circuitous route across the waters of the Cumberland, Kentucky, and Licking rivers. He came down and crossed the middle waters of the west fork of the Big

Sandy, spending the period from June 6 to
June 19, 1750, in exploring the valley. His
route, an Indian trail, led him down Paint
Creek in Johnson County, across the Big
Sandy and over the divide to the waters of
the Tug Fork, which he followed to its source.[6]
Dr. Walker was the man who named the west
fork of the Big Sandy the Louisa River, this
occurring, according to his journal, on Thursday, June 7, 1750.

During the early days of exploration and
settlement, and indeed as late as 1835, this
major stream went by the name of the Louisa
River; but shortly thereafter it became cor-
rupted into Levisa, which is now its official
designation, though occasionally, even at the
present, it is called the Louisa River. It is said
that Levisa is a colloquialization of the two
French words Le Visa, meaning the picture or
design. Tradition has it that an early French
trader,[7] whose own name has long since been
forgotten, was prompted to name the Big Sandy
River "Le Visa" because of the numerous
Indian paintings of birds and beasts which he
found on trees and rocks throughout the valley
from Paint Creek to the headwaters. The story
may seem an artful bit of fancy supported
somewhat by fact, but "Levisa" is now the

accepted name of the principal fork of the Big Sandy River, however it came about. On Mitchell's map of Kentucky and Tennessee, published in 1832, the two main headwater streams of the west fork of the Big Sandy River are named the Louisa Fork and the Russell Fork.

In 1751, Christopher Gist, in the exploratory employ of the Ohio Land Company, left the Shawnee villages at the mouth of the Scioto and came southward into Kentucky. Following the Warrior's and other trails and various water courses he finally reached the headwaters of the north fork of the Kentucky River which he was forced to ascend in order to cross the great topographic barrier of southeastern Kentucky—the Pine Mountain. On Monday, April 1, 1851, he finally crossed over from the Kentucky River to the head of Elkhorn Creek, a northeastward flowing tributary of the Russell Fork of the Big Sandy River and stood below "Pound Gap" of Pine Mountain. The finding of this important gap, of which he had no doubt already been advised by his Shawnee friends, is best told in his own language as set down in his journal:[8]

"Monday April 1—Set out the same Course about 20 M. Part of the Way we went along a

Path up the Side of a little Creek, at the Head of which was a Gap in the Mountains, then our Path went down another Creek to a Lick where Blocks of Coal about 8 or 10 in: square lay upon the Surface of the Ground, here we killed a Bear and encamped.'' This encampment was on the north fork of the Pound River, a tributary of the Russell Fork in what is now Wise County, Virginia. It was evidently a great hunting-ground, for on the following day Gist killed a buffalo, and on the third day traversed ''a small Creek on which was a large Warriors Camp that would contain 70 or 80 Warriors, their Captain's Name or Title was the Crane, as I knew by his Picture or Arms painted on a Tree.''

This camp, it is now generally agreed, was Indian Creek, the middle fork of Pound River. Passing over the head of Indian Creek, possibly by ''Indian Gap,'' Gist left the Big Sandy Valley and came down to the Clinch, up which he passed to the Blue Stone River, a tributary of the New River. The meagre details of his journal are sufficient to picture the natural ruggedness of this southwestern headwaters portion of the Big Sandy Valley and enable the reader to identify without doubt many of the points along the route which was actually traversed. Coal, the great mineral resource of this eastern portion of Kentucky, was frequently found, and we may assume used by this intrepid explorer. His specific reference to a path up either side of the Pine Mountain through the Pound Gap indicates that at this remote time, and who shall say how long previously, the Pound Gap, an ancient and abandoned stream course, was the principal pass in this region across the otherwise almost insurmountable Pine Mountain.

Dr. Walker and Captain Gist fortunately completed their explorations without molestation by the Indians, although their marauding activities in the middle of the eighteenth century, were widely extended. The Shawnee Indians and their allies in Ohio and Kentucky finally became so open in their hostility to the outlying and unprotected settlements of Virginia that the situation was unbearable. As an act of reprisal, Governor Dinwiddie ordered into the Big Sandy Valley a military movement, in 1756, that later became known as "the Sandy Creek expedition." It was designed to punish the Shawnee tribes, and to establish a well protected fort and trading post at the mouth of the Big Sandy. Although these results were not accomplished, the information

gained by Colonel Andrew Lewis and Colonel
William Preston, respectively at the time a
major and captain, was invaluable. Preston
wrote in his journal: "The creek has been
frequented by Indians both in traveling and in
hunting on it, etc."[9] In later years, after
Colonel Preston had become the surveyor and
commander of the military forces of Fincastle
County, he used his personally acquired information of the Big Sandy Valley to the
greatest advantage in protecting the settlers in
southwestern Virginia.

SWIFT'S SILVER MINES

There is a tradition commonly found
throughout the Big Sandy Valley and elsewhere in Eastern Kentucky and the adjacent
Appalachian States of Pennsylvania, West
Virginia, Virginia, Tennessee, and the Carolinas
that an English gentleman of education and
means, by the name of John Swift, came into
this portion of Kentucky annually from 1760
to 1769 at the head of a composite company of
Englishmen, Frenchmen, and Shawnee Indians
for the purpose of operating certain silver
mines. During the course of his movements
and operations through eastern Kentucky he
kept, it is asserted, a journal of his activities,

which in his old age came into the possession of a Mrs. Renfro of Bean's Station, in Eastern Tennessee. The movements of Swift and his companions were well known to his contemporaries, and so it developed, following his death, that many copies of his journal were made from time to time by those who sought to trace out his reported mines and caches of precious pig metal.

As might be expected, not one of these copies of Swift's Journal agree with any of the others, each apparently being an abbreviated interpretation of the original or some other copy. Of all of these, one copy, which belonged to Robert Alley,[10] a native of east Tennessee, but a resident of Johnson County, Kentucky, from 1859 to his death—about 1890, had the appearance of the original Swift document. Its completeness also favored Alley's contention that it was genuine. He refused to allow a complete copy of this journal to be made, but gave permission for the copying of certain portions, according to which it appears[11] that John Swift, accompanied by five men, named Hazlitt, Ireland, Blackburn, McClintock, and Staley, made their first preliminary journey into eastern Kentucky in the spring of 1860 to make arrangements to work silver mines supposed to be in that region.

They built a furnace and burned charcoal somewhere near the "Breaks of the Big Sandy" River, and then after proceeding southwestwardly along the base of Pine Mountain, where they made other mineral investigations, they returned to Alexandria, Virginia, on December 10, 1760. It appears that they had connections in Virginia with a gentleman by the name of Montgomery, who owned and operated sailing vessels to the Spanish seas and was further engaged in the work of engraving and cutting dies for the coinage of silver and gold, he being an expert in this trade, having formerly worked in the Royal Mint in the Tower of London.

Following a re-organization of the company along partnership lines, in which it appears there were fifteen participants, Swift took out a large pack train from Alexandria on the 25th of June, 1761, and following the Indian trails to the west arrived finally at the forks of the Big Sandy River, where the company was divided into two parties, one going to each of the locations selected during the previous year. Success attended this wilderness enterprise, and leaving some of the party to continue the development in Kentucky, Swift with some companions returned to the East, arriving at

THE RUGGED ELKHORN

Flowing to the northeast along the northern flank of Pine Mountain, Elkhorn Creek has a primitive beauty once common in the upper Big Sandy Valley.

Alexandria on December 2, 1761. Here they found their vessels profitably returned from the Spanish seas, and after enlarging this portion of their enterprise by the purchase of five more ships, they returned to the interior in the last week of March in 1762, going by the way of Fort Pitt, where a large pack train was taken out.

On their arrival again at the forks of the Big Sandy River they cast lots to see who should go to the various points and work their properties. Continuing on separately they found that much had been accomplished during their absence, but that the men were discouraged with the living conditions in the Kentucky wilderness. After checking up all of their affairs in the Big Sandy Valley and elsewhere, Swift and some others returned to Virginia the 1st day of September, 1762, where again they ascertained a profitable shipping experience and made preparations for increasing their operations back of the Blue Ridge and Allegheny Mountains in the wilderness of eastern Kentucky.

A further perusal of the principal statements contained in the Alley manuscript of John Swift discloses the fact that each succeeding year up to and including 1769, when it was finally determined to close down all operations and get out of the business, saw a virtual repetition of the operations of Swift and his associates as conducted from 1760 to 1762. The enterprise in which they were engaged, whatever it may actually have been, was carefully maintained and guarded at the time, and has remained a mystery down to the present. Reports of the existence of Swift's silver mines have been accredited to Johnson County, Floyd County, and Pike County in the Big Sandy Valley.

During the latter part of the eighteenth century and the first half of the nineteenth, many residents of the Big Sandy Valley and elsewhere devoted years of ceaseless labor and many thousands of dollars in an endeavor to find the exact location of the reported Swift silver mines, and though an occasional bar of silver or lead has been found in eastern Kentucky, no actual mines have ever been discovered. At several points in eastern Kentucky, however, in the Big Sandy, the Kentucky, and the Cumberland River valleys purported remains of old furnaces have been found, suggesting the operations of Europeans in this section of the State at an early date.

A review of all available data in connection with the traditions of the Swift silver mines, coupled with the geologic fact that silver mines in such fabulously paying quantities as the Swift mines are accredited to have been, have never been discovered yet in any part of the Appalachian coal field, much less in Kentucky, leads to the opinion that Swift's report was a great personal fabrication. It is held that these stories of silver mines were really invented to cover his operations while he and his fellows were engaged in the spurious minting of silver and gold bullion into English currency. The source of the crude precious metal of the counterfeiters was, of course, none other than their piratical sailing adventures on the Spanish seas.

If this interpretation is correct, it may well be, as the old tradition runs, that the mythical "great Shawnee Cave" near the "Breaks" in the Big Sandy Valley is a treasure house of silver and gold coins awaiting the coming of some unknown Aladdin. That Swift really had no silver mines in Kentucky is of little consequence as compared to the fact that he and his fellows formed a band of hardy and courageous explorers who repeatedly visited the Big Sandy Valley and eastern Kentucky prior to the Revolutionary War, and carried back to the civilization of the Atlantic Coast a diversified and accurate knowledge of that unknown western country which is now eastern Kentucky.

THE WASHINGTON SURVEY

Colonel George Washington, who had seen much service in the French and Indian engagements west of the Appalachian Mountains, and was quite as well informed as any of the colonists of his time with respect to these new lands in the Ohio Valley, is believed by many to have made the first survey in the Big Sandy Valley, and probably in Kentucky. From 1767 to 1770 he was engaged in the exploration of the region adjoining the Ohio, the lower Kanawha, and the Big Sandy Rivers. During this period he is credited with having surveyed for one John Fry under the Proclamation of 1763 a tract of 2,084 acres located on both sides of the Big Sandy River, including the present townsite of Louisa. Whether Washington himself or a designated assistant made this Big Sandy survey may never be definitely proven, though much time and money have been expended in the attempt by historical organizations and interested individuals in Kentucky and elsewhere. The fact remains, despite a very considerable contrary proof, that the surveyor, if indeed it were not Washington, marked this survey, which was a very accurate one, and on the beginning cornerstone cut the initials, G. W. The Honorable Richard Apperson, of Mt. Sterling, Kentucky, lately deceased, some years ago held the original patent to this Big Sandy tract. It was granted in 1792.[12] Mr. F. T. D. Wallace, long an honored resident of Louisa, has recently told the writer that he remembers the Washington-Fry Survey well, having been engaged in re-running it when a young man, at which time he saw the corners all marked as described.

BOONE AND OTHER HUNTERS

While this survey in the lower part of the Big Sandy Valley was engaging the attention of Washington, it has recently been shown that Daniel Boone,[13] the popular hero of Kentucky discovery and settlement, in company with William Hill, spent the winter of 1767 and 1768 exploring, hunting and camping on the upper waters of the Big Sandy. Boone, who was in search of the rich land reported to be located in Kentucky, had crossed over the headwaters of the Big Sandy, and, somewhat discouraged by the rough nature of the country he encountered in what is now Pike

and Floyd counties, went into camp at a salt
lick located about ten miles west of Prestonsburg on Left Middle Creek. Game was plentiful, and all Boone and his companion had to do
was to await at their little shack the coming of
the deer and buffalo to lick the salt. Their discovery of this salt lick was of inestimable value
to them, for with the scant supply of ammunition at their disposal, they were thus able to
husband their stores and tide over the hard
months of the enforced winter encampment. It
is not at all improbable that this salt lick played
an important part in saving the lives of both
of these hardy woodsmen, and enabled Boone
to return to the Yadkin, and later take part in
the well known explorations led by Findley
through Cumberland Gap into the Bluegrass
region in 1769.

Although Boone had been in Kentucky, he
did not know it. His recollections of that
winter of 1767 spent in the rugged hills of what
is now Floyd County were unpleasant. There
can be no doubt but that many who otherwise
would have come down to the headwaters of the
Big Sandy through the passes well marked by
the Indian trails (later known as the Tug, Dry
Fork, and Levisa Fork gaps), were turned
away by the advice of Boone, and his family

and their friends. Felix Walker, who with Captain Twetty and six others started in February, 1775, to explore the Leowvisay (Levisa) country (now Kentucky), met Colonel Richard Henderson negotiating his treaty at Watauga. After the treaty had been agreed upon, these explorers joined hands with Henderson and came over into the central portion of this State.[14] A real exploring and bear hunting party composed of William Thornton, James Fowler, and William Pittman, did, however, cross over from the Clinch River into the headwaters of the Big Sandy, and passing through Pound and Shelby gaps continued down Shelby Creek, thence over ridges to a stream where they discovered the old salt springs at the mouth of a small creek, which later took the name of Salt Lick Creek. Fowler, who was evidently an ardent and successful hunter, called the main stream of this region Beaver Creek,[15] and it has held the name ever since. The Thornton party did not cross the Levisa Fork of Big Sandy at all, but returned to Virginia unmindful of the rich bottom lands which they had so nearly penetrated. In March, 1796, William Thornton again came to this lick, accompanied by Philip Roberts, to secure salt for the settlements.

Toward the close of the eighteenth century the Big Sandy Valley had been sufficiently explored to allow a fairly accurate though general description of the region. Though the ways and means of securing information concerning the western country was for the most part indirect at the time, it is surprising how well done many of the descriptions were. Gilbert Imlay in 1797 says:[16] "Totteroy falls into the Ohio on the same side (as the Kanawha) and is passable with boats to the mountains. It is long, and has not many branches, interlocks with Red Creek, or Clinch's River (a branch of Cuttawa). It has below the mountains, especially for 15 miles from the mouth, very good land. And here is a visible effect of the difference of climate from the upper parts of Ohio. Here the long reed or Carolina cane grows in plenty, even upon the upland, and the severity of the winter does not kill them; so that travelers this way are not obliged to provide any winter support for their horses. And the same holds all the way down Ohio, especially on the southeast side to the Falls and thence on both sides."

NOTES TO CHAPTER II

[1] LaSalle and the Discovery of the Great West. Parkman, pp. 19-36.

AN OLD GRIST MILL

Though most of the corn during the period of settlement was ground in hand and water mills, there were a few horse mills such as this on Abner Branch of Left Beaver Creek, Floyd County.

[2] First Explorations of the Trans-Allegheny Region by the Virginians. Alvord & Bidgood, pp. 196-205.

[3] First Explorations of the Trans-Allegheny Region by the Virginians. Alvord & Bidgood, pp. 210-226.

[4] The Discovery of Kentucky. Jillson, Register of the Kentucky State Historical Society, Vol. 20, No. 59, pp. 117-129, May, 1922.

[5] First Report, Department of Archives and History of West Virginia. V. A. Lewis, Vol. I, pp. 156-158.

[6] First Explorations of Kentucky (Walker's Journal). Johnston, pp. 67-80.

[7] Trans-Allegheny Pioneers. John P. Hale.

[8] Journal of Christopher Gist in "First Explorations of Kentucky." Johnston, p. 155.

[9] History of Tazewell County and Southwest Virginia. Pendleton, p. 218.

[10] History of Kentucky. Kerr, Vol. I, p. 130.

[11] History of Kentucky. Kerr, Vol. I, p. 131.

[12] L. C. Draper Manuscript, 5C 38. Personal letter from Richard Apperson, dated Mt. Sterling, Ky., May 29, 1854. Archives Wisconsin Historical Society; also History of Kentucky. Collins, Vol. 2, pp. 368 and 460. Also "On the Storied Ohio." Thwaites, p. 141. Also Early Western Travels. Thwaites, Vol. IV (footnote), p. 155. Also Scrapbook, Robertson, p. 271.

[13] First Explorations of Daniel Boone in Kentucky. Jillson, Register of the Kentucky State Historical Society, Vol. 20, No. 59, pp. 204-206, May, 1922. Also the Boone Family. Spraker, p. 73, 1922.

[14] The Wilderness Road. Speed, p. 31.

[15] History of Kentucky. Collins, Vol. II, pp. 237-238.

[16] A Topographical Description of the Western Territory of North America. Imlay, p. 116.

CHAPTER III

BORDER WARFARE

(1750-1795)

Toward the middle of the eighteenth century the various Indian tribes occupying the Ohio, Tennessee, and Mississippi river valleys began to view with increasing alarm and sullen chagrin the growing pressure of the white settlers from the east. Time and again as they were forced to vacate and abandon forever their favorite and traditional hunting-grounds, the spirit of revenge arose within them. They were not long in recognizing the advancing English settler as a land thief, nor slow in retaliating with the same principle of outlawry, which at first consisted chiefly in plundering the whites for desirable military and domestic stores. When the settler resisted, hatred flamed high in the savage breast, and deeds of blood and cruelty so terrible as to beggar description became commonplace.

In the year 1754 the French and Indian War began in earnest. Marauding parties of Indians from the Ohio River villages made their way over war trails leading through the

Ohio, Kanawha, and Big Sandy valleys. They
came down from ambush on the outlying
settlers at many a point in southwestern Virginia, burning the cabins, scalping the helpless
women and children, and carrying the men off
into captivity. The horror and the hopeless-
ness of the times were widespread. The defeat
of the crown and colonial forces under General
Braddock at the hands of the combined French
and Indians in 1755, left the western portions
of Pennsylvania, Maryland, and Virginia without any protection from the bloodthirsty
savages. The contemporaneous correspond-
ence of Col. Washington, who as a colonial
officer was an eye witness to the fateful rout
of Braddock, reflects with what degree of alarm
farsighted Englishmen of that time viewed the
prospect in the "back country."

The Draper Massacre

The massacre in 1755 at Draper's meadows,
now Montgomery County, Virginia, in which
Mrs. Mary Ingles, her two little boys, and her
sister, Mrs. Draper, were taken prisoners by
the Shawnee Indians is typical of the times.
The captives were taken to the Indian village
at the mouth of the Scioto River, where they
were subjected to great cruelties, including the

running of the gauntlet. Later Mrs. Ingles
escaped while engaged in making salt at Big
Bone Lick. Threading her way eastward along
the south shore of the Ohio with an elderly
Dutch woman who had been a prisoner for a
long time, she finally came to the Big Sandy
Valley. They were undoubtedly the first white
women to penetrate this region.

The river was in flood, and the two women
were required to ascend until a crossing could
be made on drift wood. The small amount of
Indian corn they had carried with them was
soon exhausted, and for more than a month they
lived on such wild berries and roots as they
could find. Early winter with snow came. At
last, faint and exhausted from hunger and
exposure, and in a most desperate plight, they
made their way to a cabin of friends on the
upper Kanawha. Mr. William Ingles, her
husband, started out at once with a searching
party, but one of his boys died before he could
be reached, and the other was not found
and returned until fifteen years after the
massacre.[1]

THE SANDY CREEK VOYAGE

It was the repetition of such bloody affairs
as that which was visited on the Ingles family

that finally caused Governor Dinwiddie of Virginia to send out the "Sandy Creek Voyage" on February 18, 1756, under the leadership of Colonel (then Major) Andrew Lewis. Colonel George Washington, then the commander of all the Virginia military forces named Major Lewis to head the expedition. The command was made up principally of about 400 backwoodsmen and a few Cherokee and Chickasaw Indians who had been induced to become allies of the English settlers. Captain William Preston was placed in charge of the vanguard, and the march began from Camp Frederick in what is now Pulaski County, Virginia. Although the men were well acquainted with the Indian style of fighting, Washington appreciated better than Governor Dinwiddie the naturally severe handicaps the colony forces would have to meet, and steadfastly opposed the plan.

The purpose of the expedition was to march down the Big Sandy to the Ohio River, and thence to the several Shawnee villages which were to be destroyed. The expedition started in good spirits, but the limited food supply and the heavy rains of the season disheartened and disorganized the men. After crossing the Holston and the Clinch rivers they passed

over the divide of the Tug Fork and started
down the Big Sandy Valley. On March 2nd,
when about sixty miles of the journey had been
traversed, Major Lewis and his command came
in contact with the Indians. The wily savages
did not engage the expedition in a large
encounter, but drew them on, allowing growing
hunger and fatigue to weaken the Lewis command. On the 13th of March at a point
somewhere near the mouth of Rockcastle Creek
on the Tug Fork, the men refused to proceed
any further. The entreaties of Colonel Lewis
were in vain. The volunteers started the disorganized return, and the conditions were so
bad that Captain William Preston wrote in his
Journal, "That any man in camp would have
ventured his life for a supper."

Retreating upstream, provisions became
completely exhausted, and the men were actually
starving. The weather was extremely cold,
and a heavy snow fell during the march. They
stopped at the Burning Spring, a natural gas
seepage, near Warfield, and taking strips of
the hides of buffalo they had left there, broiled
them for food. The cutting of these strips or
thugs gave the Tug River its name. On leaving
this point the men scattered through the mountains, attempting to reach the settlements by

some short cut. In such a predicament, many
of them perished, either freezing or starving
to death, or killed by their savage enemies.
The failure of the Sandy Creek expedition
was not only a sad blow to the settlements along
the New River, but soon proved a great warring
incentive to the Shawnees and other hostile
tribes of the Ohio Valley. They continued their
savage attacks on the border settlements, and
extended their scalping and pillaging excursions
into the villages of the Holston and Potomac.
In these engagements they were generously
encouraged and supported by the French, who
were at that time at war with Great Britain.
The French provided them with arms, ammunition, and other supplies, and paid a liberal
bounty for English scalps. The awful carnage
wrought by the savages continued until the
autumn of 1765, when two treaties were made
with the Indians, one at Niagara, and one at
Muskingum, thus closing the French and Indian
War. Through the Muskingum treaty, which
was negotiated by Colonel Bouquet with the
Delawares and Shawnees, two hundred and
eighty-four prisoners, ninety from Virginia and
one hundred and sixteen from Pennsylvania,
were returned to their homes.[2] During this
period the Big Sandy Valley had been used to

great advantage by the red man as a warring basis for his depredations, and few white men with the exception of John Swift and his men, dared to enter it. Painted warriors infested every river trail and pass. Records of the times were few and poorly kept, but they are sufficient to show the troublous nature of the times and region. In 1764 marauding Indians suddenly came out of the Big Sandy Valley and devastated outlying settlements over a widespread area of southwestern Virginia.[3] Again in 1774 numerous scalping parties used the Big Sandy Valley as a warpath to penetrate into that region.[4]

Lord Dunmore's War

The culmination of these incessant Indian hostilities, and the great carnage and terror which they spread through the country, resulted in Lord Dunmore's decision to bring about a decisive engagement and a lasting peace with the Indians. In carrying out this expedition the backwoods militia of southwestern Virginia played a leading part. The battle took place at Point Pleasant, the juncture of the Kanawha and Ohio rivers, and under the direction of Colonel Lewis and Lord Dunmore was thoroughly decisive. The engagement started

THE "POUND GAP"

Above the placid waters of a little artificial lake on the head of Elkhorn Creek one may see this famous "wind gap", in Pine Mountain. It was a pass well known to the buffalo, the Indian, and pioneer.

Monday, October 10, 1774. During the early part of the battle it appeared as though the Indians would gain the upper hand, but a skillful flanking movement executed by a young lieutenant, Isaac Shelby, who was to be a few years later the first Governor of Kentucky, defeated the savages and put them to rout. So quickly effected was the Indian retreat, that many of the white officers could not believe they had really withdrawn. But the warriors were disheartened and quite ready to quit fighting. The crafty chief Cornstalk saw the uselessness of the Indian's attempt to keep the white settler out of the Ohio Valley. His proposals bore fruit. The Indian forces, composed chiefly of the Shawnee and their allied tribes, were demoralized, and a lasting treaty was concluded by Lord Dunmore.[5]

REVOLUTIONARY WAR REPRISALS

The decisive defeat of the Indians at Point Pleasant and their consequent humiliation had hardly begun to be felt, however, when the Revolutionary War began in 1776. During the five years which followed, the British became the chief supporters of the relentless savages, and from their posts in the Ohio Valley sent many a marauding party into southwestern Virginia. The Big Sandy Valley continued to prove a convenient field base for the savages, and as late as March, 1781, scalping parties came across the Big Sandy trail to burn and pillage in the Holston River settlements. Captives were taken, and the new country was thrown into great confusion.[6] Though a treaty of peace was negotiated by Colonels Campbell, Martin, Shelby, and Sevier, British agents continued to urge the Indians in their depredations. The records of the Clinch Valley tell of numerous massacres of settlers and white hunters on the headwaters of Sandy and in the Clinch River valleys even to September, 1784.

Though organized invasions of central Kentucky ceased about 1783, small predatory bands of Indians made the outlying settler's life unsafe for still another decade in every part of the new territory.[7] Daring English hunters penetrating into the headwaters of the Big Sandy in the autumn of 1785 saw everywhere signs of warring and scalping parties of Indians, who still made their bloody forays into the Clinch River Valley through this convenient pass.[8]

Indian Outrages and Defeat

In 1787 Jennie Wiley, wife of an outlying settler, Thomas Wiley, in Abb's Valley, was captured by a mixed band of Cherokees and Shawnees. While her family was being massacred, she was dragged away, her captors leading her into the Big Sandy Valley and almost to the mouth of the Scioto on the Ohio before they turned back to a temporary encampment near the mouth of Mud Lick Creek in Johnson County. From this camp, after many hardships and privations, she escaped in the night to the recently erected Harman's Station, just below the mouth of Johns Creek in the Levisa River bottom land.[9] From this point Mrs. Wiley made her way back in safety to her husband; and years later both returned to the Big Sandy, where they took up their residence and started life anew near the mouth of Toms Creek in what is now Johnson County.

About the time of the Wiley massacre the depredations of the Indians became so widespread and terrible that the settlers occupying Harman Station were forced to flee back to the older settlements. The violence of the Indians did not cease, and as soon as Harman's Station was abandoned, it was

burned to the ground. In 1790 the block-
house which Charles Vancouver, a Londoner,
and his party had erected during February and
March, 1779, on the point between the Tug and
Levisa Forks of the Big Sandy, had to be
abandoned. Again, the whites had no sooner
left than the Indians came down upon it and
burned it, leaving but a pile of smouldering
ashes to mark its location.[10]   Finally General
Anthony Wayne's victory at Fallen Timbers,
near Toledo, August 3, 1795, was followed with
a treaty of peace with the Northwest Indians
made at Greenville, Ohio, August 20, which
relieved Kentucky from any further defensive
and offensive warfare against the red men.[11]
The Big Sandy Valley, the last warring strong-
hold in eastern Kentucky, was thus thrown
open to settlement.

The Spanish Intrigues

While the increasing hostility of the Indian
tribes was the great problem of the "back
country" during the latter part of the eighteenth century, stirring events were taking place
at home and abroad which directly involved eastern Kentucky. Along the Atlantic seaboard the
Revolutionary War was dragging on to its
wearisome end. Washington was playing for

Cornwallis at Yorktown. The Continental Congress had ceased to exist, except in name. Dr. Benjamin Franklin was in Paris urging a larger assistance from France. National recognition by Spain was regarded as necessary to the solution of the problems of the infant United States. It was held that Spanish approval would bring about a like attitude on the part of France and other European nations, thus ending the war.

During the years 1779-1780 John Jay was sent as minister plenipotentiary to the Court at Madrid to arrange this difficult matter. Spain, fully aware of the strength of her position, made a bold play for the entire Mississippi Valley. At this point, had it not been for the patience and high patriotism of John Jay, it is very probable that during the period of its early settlement at least, the Big Sandy Valley would have become a part of the Spanish frontier. It would have been backed by a vast Crown territory extending from the proposed Appalachian boundary of the new American Republic to the extreme southwest. The intrigues of the allies, France and Spain, during the latter part of the American Revolution led Don Diego de Gardoqui, the Spanish charge d'affaires, to contend ''that the ter-

ritory of the United States should extend no
farther west than the settlements permitted by
the proclamation of (the English King George
of October 7th) 1763; that the United States
thus having no territory upon the Mississippi,
had no right to navigate that stream . . . ."12

Though news traveled slowly in those days,
it was not long before the settlers in Kentucky
and Tennessee learned that the pressure of the
seven northern States for a commercial and
political treaty with Spain had forced Jay
unwillingly to propose that the United States
waive its navigation rights to the Mississippi
for a period of twenty-five years. Prompt and
forceful action on the part of the western
frontiersmen was impossible, but their violent
resentment soon found its way to the East. In
this time of crisis Jay decided that a treaty
which lacked the support of the people most
affected would be worse than none at all. He,
therefore, immediately withdrew all of his
proposals to Madrid and leaving that country
joined John Adams at Paris. Jay did not know
it then, but Spain was simply using the
"Mississippi Navigation Proposals" to alienate
the people of Kentucky and Tennessee from
the new union of thirteen original States. His

sagacity it now appears was quite the equal of the secret diplomacy of the old world courts.

It had been the plan of Vergennes, the French Secretary of State, to give Spain everything south of 31° N. Lat. and west of the Alleghenys, or at the farthest, the Ohio River. Counts Luzerne and Aranda maintained a united insistence upon these boundary terms in the proposed treaty. Both Jay and John Adams were resolute in their opposition, though the Congress was half inclined to allow the concession. Finally by exercising an adroitness of diplomacy seldom equaled, these courageous gentlemen, joined at last by Dr. Benjamin Franklin, concluded on November 30, 1782, secret provisional articles to a treaty between Great Britain and the United States.

This treaty, which was signed September 3, 1783, nearly a year later, eliminated the restrictions of the proclamation of 1763—the Allegheny frontier—so much sought by France and Spain. By it the western boundary of Virginia was established, as far as the British were concerned, at the Mississippi River, and the Big Sandy Valley and all of Kentucky was by the terms kept open for American settlement. But the region was not freed from the prospect of Spanish provincial control. Though the

East little suspected the course of changing events in the frontier country, the sleek and artful hands of General James Wilkinson and Judge Benjamin Sebastian soon made the stage ready for the last act of this absorbing international drama in Kentucky.

The acknowledgment by England of the boundary on the west, desirable as it was, did not bring security to the settlers. Murderous Indian forays from the north continued, and though Patrick Henry, Governor of Virginia, in 1786 sought aid from Congress, the Kentuckians were finally forced to organize under the leadership of George Rogers Clark an armed resistance to the savage. The apparent lack of interest indicated by the constituted authorities of the new republic in the vital affairs of the western country, coupled with the scheming machinations of certain political adventurers, who continued to ably delineate the advantage to the Bluegrass planter of a closer union with the Spanish interests to the South, resulted in a growing feeling of unrest and dissatisfaction.

When in 1788, the Seventh Convention of Kentucky assembled at Danville, it was addressed by the disloyal General Wilkinson, a hireling of the Spanish Court. Shrewd politician that he was, he scrupled not to put Kentucky on trial as to whether it would remain an unprotected western outpost of the new United States or voluntarily detach itself from Virginia and cast its lot with the Spanish provinces to the south. The open navigation of the Mississippi River, so greatly desired by the planters of the Bluegrass as an outlet for their tobacco and other products, was offered by the Spanish Governor Miro as a first reward for the latter move.

For a day or two the political fate of Kentucky stood in the balance, while a pictured rainbow of agricultural prosperity matched its weight against that of a new patriotism. Sectional feeling ran high, involving many of the leaders of the embryo State. At length while some delegates openly favored the treasonous scheme of Wilkinson and his associates, the majority of the convention, loyal pioneers of Kentucky County, stood proudly for their place in the new American Union of States and against any illegal separation from Virginia. Good fortune had again smiled upon the rich though solitary forested hills of the Big Sandy Valley, saving it once more and for all time from the clutches of Spain. As the historic convention at Danville disbanded, adventurers, surveyors, and explorers just returned from the field were filing in tidewater Virginia the first surveys of the upper part of the Big Sandy Valley, while at each of the rock-ribbed passes at the head of the great river stood the finest Anglo-Saxon blood America has ever known, ready to claim the land and hold it by homestead.

NOTES TO CHAPTER III

[1] Tours, Croghan, in Early Western Travels. Thwaites, Vol. I, p. 134; and Travels, Nuttall, in Vol. XIII, p. 59. Also History of Kentucky. Smith, pp. 27-28. Also Sketches of Virginia, 2nd Series (footnote), pp. 150-159. Also Trans-Allegheny Pioneers. Hale, p. 29. Also Documentary History of Dunmore's War. Thwaites & Kellogg, p. 101. Also History of Kentucky. Collins, Vol. II, p. 53.

[2] History of Southwest Virginia. Summer's, p. 82.

[3] History of Southwest Virginia. Summer's, p. 81.

[4] Documentary History of Dunmore's War. Thwaites and Kellogg, p. 204. Also History of Tazewell County and Southwest Virginia. Pendleton, pp. 281, 295.

[5] Tour, Cuming, in Early Western Travels. Thwaites, Vol. IV, p. 142. Also Documentary History of Dunmore's War. Thwaites-Kellogg, pp. 9 to 28. Also History of Tazewell County and Southwest Virginia. Pendleton, p. 290.

[6] History of Southwest Virginia. Summer's, p. 349.

[7] Kentucky a Part of Virginia, Duke, in The South in the Building of the Nation, Vol. I, p. 263.

[8] History of Southwest Virginia. Summer's, p. 387.

[9] The Big Sandy Valley. Ely, pp. 450-451. Also Founding of Harman's Station. Connelley, pp. 26-92.

[10] Big Sandy Valley. Ely, pp. 11-12.

[11] Kentucky a Part of Virginia, Duke, in The South in the Building of the Nation, Vol. I, p. 263.

[12] The Spanish Conspiracy. T. M. Green, p. 19.

CHAPTER IV

LOG CABIN STRUGGLE

(1772-1820)

The great tide of immigration which flooded central and western Kentucky during the last quarter of the eighteenth century with homesteaders, spent itself in finding out the more remote areas in the mountain regions where good bottom land was available. As early as 1772 the rich river lands of the lower Big Sandy had become known in the eastern part of the Old Dominion. John Swift and his associates, for all the secrecy that attended their adventures, must have said much concerning Kentucky in the course of time. Col. Washington, who was personally interested in lower Big Sandy Valley land ventures, undoubtedly aided the spread of the news through the East, while others of whom we have no record presumably returned to praise the wilderness land of the Louisa. The earliest petition for a large land grant in the Big Sandy is that of Carter Braxton, Richard Corbin, Samuel Thompson, John Blair, Thomas Walker Gilmer and others who sought the Honorable John,

Earl of Dunmore, Royal Governor of Virginia, April 25, 1772, for 59,000 acres of land, beginning at the mouth of the Louisa River and extending along the Big Sandy to the Ohio.[1] While the interest of the land speculators centered in the lower Big Sandy Valley, the homesteaders were beginning to look with covetous eyes at the rich river and creek bottom lands farther up the Valley. In 1773 Enoch Smith, Richard Spur, John Wilkerson, and William ————, pioneering on the headwaters of Johns Creek, in what is now Pike County, built a horse pen of logs. It stood for many years. This rude shelter was located about five miles east of Pikeville, and has been used as a starting point in many of the old land surveys[2] of that vicinity. Whether they at this time built a cabin nearby and occupied their land is not revealed, but it seems doubtful, because of the hostility of the Indians then in this region.

A year later, April 29, 1774, John Floyd, who was soon to give his name to all of Eastern Kentucky, dropped down the Ohio and passed the mouth of the Big Sandy. As assistant surveyor, under Colonel William Preston of Fincastle County, he was bent on surveying new lands for Patrick Henry and others.

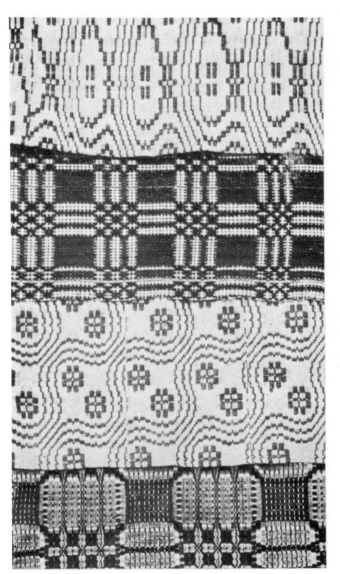

SOME BIG SANDY COVERLET PATTERNS

During the early days hand-made wool and cotton bed coverings such as these were made and used in nearly every Big Sandy household. These patterns from left to right are: (1) Sea Star, red and white; (2) Snail Trail and Cat Tracks, blue and white; (3) Doors and Windows, red and white; (4) Rattlesnake Trail, blue and white.

Colonel Floyd, who later became widely known during the celebrated Indian campaigns in central Kentucky, Indiana, and Illinois, was accompanied by a Mr. Douglas, a Kentucky explorer of experience, and by Hite Dandridge, Thomas Hanson, James Knox, Roderick McCra, and Mordecai Batson. Thomas Hanson kept a journal[3] of the expedition which throws much light on the hazardous nature of the enterprise. Colonel Floyd was well advised of the hostile activity of the Shawnees in eastern Kentucky and the Ohio bottoms, and for this reason evidently made no attempt to survey lands in the Big Sandy. His surveys were confined principally to the areas along the Ohio below the Shawnee camp at the mouth of the Scioto. In the fall of this year, after many adventures, Floyd returned to the East, where he joined the Colonial forces assembled at Point Pleasant and assisted materially in the defeat of the Indians in the Lord Dunmore campaign.

Although the Big Sandy Valley was much overrun at this time by small bands of vicious Indians, it was occasionally used of necessity by the leaders of the border militia. On June 12, 1775, Captain William Russell, stationed at Point Pleasant at the mouth of the Kanawha, dispatched a letter to Colonel William Fleming, in which, among other things, he said: "I am this morning preparing to start off our cattle up Sandy, and expect that the Command will leave this Wednesday or Thursday at farthest, and shall decamp myself with a convoy to the other Stores next Monday, and expect to overtake the stock at the Big Painted Lick (near Paintsville) about sixty miles up Sandy."[4]

THE FIRST SETTLERS

Tradition has it that among the very earliest settlers of the upper Big Sandy were "Dad" Owen, "General" Ratliff, James Honaker, and Kinsey B. Cecil, all of whom settled along the Big Sandy, near the site of Pikeville, between 1785 and 1790. In the early fall of 1787 Matthias Harman, one of the traditional "Long Hunters of Kentucky," accompanied by a party consisting of Henry Harman, Henry Skaggs, James Skaggs, Robert Hawes, some of the Damrons and a man named Draper, in all about twenty men, constructed a rude log hunting-camp in a "rock-house" on the headwaters of the Big Sandy. The camp unfortunately was located on an Indian trail, resulting shortly thereafter in bringing Harman and his men into an engagement with a mongrel band of warring Shawnee, Cherokee, and Delaware Indians. Some of the Indians were slain, and as a reprisal the savage leaders moved swiftly over the headwaters of Big Sandy, as was their common custom. There they fell upon the outlying Virginian settlements and perpetrated the Wiley massacre.[5] Harman and his companions, sensing that the Indians would seek this kind of revenge, returned home immediately, but too late to prevent the terrible atrocity. They soon organized a party and followed the savages and their captives, Mrs. Wiley and her baby, into the Big Sandy Valley. Harman intended to overtake them if possible, and if not, to establish an outpost station in the Big Sandy which would discourage further depredations by the marauding Shawnees and their allies in the Clinch and Holston river settlements. After following the trail of the Indians several days, Harman and his companions lost it in the flood waters of the Levisa Fork.

HARMAN'S STATION ESTABLISHED

Then prospecting the country carefully, they finally selected a site in the Big Sandy bottoms just below the mouth of Johns Creek, and erected, in the fall and winter of 1787 and

1788, a log fort, which became known as Harman's Station. This was the first English outpost in the Big Sandy Valley of which there is a definite record.[6] It was to this block house that Jennie Wiley fled after her escape from the Indians on Mud Lick Creek. Had it not been erected, it is altogether likely that Mrs. Wiley would never have made good her escape from the savages, or lived to tell the terrible tale of her captivity. In the winter of 1789 Indian reprisals were continuously directed against this outlying English block house, and the Harmans were forced to abandon it.

The Shawnees looked with great disfavor upon the attempts of the Harmans, and the subsequent attempts of Vancouver and his party, to establish themselves on the Big Sandy. Not only were these settlements spoiling one of the last large hunting-grounds of the Indians, but they were barring the only through and direct route available to the Shawnees leading to the growing settlements on the Holston and Clinch rivers to the southeast. With the warring trails up the Big Sandy Valley permanently closed to them, the sagacious Indian chiefs saw that in the near future their reprisals upon the rich English settlements would end. The settlers also saw the certain advantages of acquiring the Big Sandy Valley, and in the year 1790, Harman's Station at the mouth of Johns Creek was rebuilt, never again to be given up to the Indians.

LOCATION OF PRESTON'S STATION

In 1791 John Spurlock erected the first permanent house where Prestonsburg now stands. The temporary camps of John Graham and other Virginia surveyors had preceded him, but to him belongs the credit of being the first to build his home in this locality. Spurlock's settlement being the earliest in point of time, gives Prestonsburg the distinction of being the oldest town on the Big Sandy River. The original cabin built by John Spurlock, the pioneer, stood for many years as a landmark in the "back-from-the-river" part of Prestonsburg, near the present residence of Mr. J. M. Davidson. Closely following Spurlock came a number of other families, and within a year or so the place became known as Preston's Station. It was so called in honor of John Preston of Augusta County, Virginia. He had been a member of the Virginia Legislature and was for many years the Treasurer of the Old Dominion. He came from a notable line of Londonderry-Irish ancestry, his father having been Col.

William Preston of border warfare fame. His grandfather, John Preston, the emigrant, a man of means and culture, came to America from Ireland in 1740 and settled in Augusta County, Virginia.[7]

John Preston in company with John Graham was interested in several large grants in this vicinity. One of these, known later as the Osborn tract, situated in the bottoms of Middle Creek near the Sandy River, was surveyed for Preston by John Graham December 24, 1787. Graham himself owned in fee a large portion of the land on which Prestonsburg is now located, and on June 26, 1815, he sold all the ground for the streets and alleys and the courthouse square of this town to the county of Floyd for the nominal consideration of one dollar. There is little evidence that John Preston cared much for this wilderness country which so early in its history honored him. He made Harry Stratton his agent in the Big Sandy Valley, and subsequently transferred all of his principal surveys to John Graham.

In the year 1799 Preston's Station became known as Prestonsburg, and was made the county seat of the newly created Floyd County, which then comprised all the eastern portion of the State. John Graham, who had been the

Deputy Surveyor of Mason County, Kentucky, when this Ohio River county included the entire Sandy Valley, produced the first map of Prestonsburg in 1797, prior to the erection of Floyd County. After the organization of the new county this map was filed in the records of the county clerk, where it was destroyed by fire in 1808 when the first Floyd County Court House burned. In 1810 a duplicate of the original plat of the town of Prestonsburg was made a part of the Floyd County records by order of the Floyd Court. This court was apparently both a circuit and county court (App. D) during these early times. John Graham and Alexander Lackey were the judges.

The Pioneer Leader

John Graham, who was born in Augusta County, Virginia, January 1, 1765, was the one real leader in the Valley during the period of its early settlement. He had seen service in the Eighth Virginia Regiment on the Continental line during the Revolution, and with Virginia Treasury warrants had made large purchases of lands in the Big Sandy. Of a versatile temperament he was, at various times, soldier, explorer, surveyor, landowner, merchant, banker, judge and representative from

Mason County at Frankfort. Such varied activities, characteristically early American, were quite as much a product of the times as the man. Yet it must be said in all fairness that John Graham, like other Kentucky pioneers of exceptional ability, recognized and took advantage of his civic responsibilities and regional opportunities as they presented themselves. Therein lay the secret of the personal success which made him in his latter years not only a very wealthy and highly respected gentleman, but the largest individual land owner of eastern Kentucky. Educated in the Old Dominion, he possessed withal an attractive and cultured personality, which, coupled with a wide reputation for personal fearlessness and achievement, made him decidedly the outstanding figure of his time in the Big Sandy Valley. Though a hundred years have now passed and no direct descendant lives to perpetuate the line of this illustrious pioneer, tradition colorful and quaint in the ''Sandy Country'' still honors the name of John Graham.

THE GREAT INVASION

About 1792, Vancouver's Station, which had been destroyed by the Indians in 1790, was re-established on the tongue of land between

AN OLD TIME VIEW OF PRESTONSBURG

Although the first county seat town on the Big Sandy River, Prestonsburg had but two or three streets and twenty or thirty buildings, including the court house and jail, in 1850. This view, characteristic of the "old town," during the period of this history, is from the west side of "Sandy," looking north down Second Street. It was taken by R. C. B. Thruston in 1887.

the Levisa and Tug forks of the Big Sandy.[8]
A few years later this settlement was known
as "Balchlutha," and is so designated on the
early maps of the State.[9]

In 1789 the Leslies attempted to make a
settlement at the mouth of Paint Creek on
the Tug River, but were driven out by the
vigilance of the Indians. They returned,
however, in 1791; but instead of locating on
Pond Creek, they crossed over on to Johns
Creek, and formed what was later known as
the Leslie Settlement. About this time came
the Damrons, Harmans, Auxiers, Grahams,
Browns, Marcums, Johns, Hammonds, Wed-
dingtons, Morgans, Harrises, Pinsons, Walkers,
Williamsons, Marrs, Mayos, Lackeys, Laynes,
Prestons, Boarders and many others.[10] In 1793
the Big Sandy and adjacent regions of eastern
Kentucky, while legally a part of Mason
County, Kentucky, had already become known
as District No. 1, Floyd County. The rapidity
with which this section was being settled can be
inferred from the fact that during the three
years which had elapsed since the re-establish-
ment of Harman Station in 1790 at least four
hundred and thirty families and four hundred
and forty-eight male whites above the age of
twenty-one chargeable with tax were resident
settlers in this section.

The following men were residents of Floyd County—essentially the Big Sandy region—in 1793.[11] Assuming three or four to a family, there were therefore not more than about 1,500 souls in the entire Valley at that time:

A

Abbot, Joseph
Adamson, Andrew
Adamson, John
Aikins, Gabriel
Aikins, Richard
Allen, Barnibas
Allen, Joseph

Allen, Natha
Allison, John
Aplegate, Richard
Archer, Benjamin
Armstrong, John
Ayers, Richard

B

Bagby, Robert
Baker, Joshua
Baker, Wiliam
Baley, Grombright
Baley, Henry
Barackman, Jacob
Barkley, James
Barr, Margit
Bartle, John
Bayles, Daniel
Beale, John
Bellvil, Samuel
Belt, John
Bennitt, Elisha
Bennum, Robert
Berry, Elijah
Berry, Henry
Berry, William
Black, James
Black, John
Blanchard, John
Blasher, Henry
Blasingam, James
Boyd, John

Boyd, Thomas
Boyd, Thomas, Jr.
Boyd, William
Brannan, Alex
Brannan, David
Braughtem, Benjamin
Briant, Presley
Brinson, Thomas
Brosheres, Thomas
Brown, Grier
Brown, John
Brown, Joseph
Brown, Robert
Brown, Vincent
Brown, William
Browning, Basil
Bruner, John
Buchanan, William
Buckanan, Alex
Buckingham, Enoch
Buckler, Stephen
Burous, Waters
Byland, Samuel

C

Callan, William
Calvin, James
Calvin, Luther
Calvin, Stephen
Campbell, Francis
Campbell, John
Campbell, Johnston
Camron, Daniel
Cane, Dennis
Carbry, John
Carpenter, Richard
Carter, James
Cartmall, Samuel
Case, Goldsmith
Chambers, William
Chinworth, Abraham
Chinworth, Arthur
Chinworth, Elijah
Chinworth, John
Chinworth, Thomas
Clemon, John
Clemons, Joseph

Clerk, James
Clerk, William
Combs, Joseph
Conrey, John
Conrey, Jonathan
Coopper, Vincent
Cook, Catherine
Courent, William
Courne, John
Covert, John
Cox, Jacob
Crabb, Faney
Craig, Heathey
Craig, Servis
Crane, Elihu
Crosey, Moses
Crosley, William
Crute, John
Cuppy, Henry
Curtis, George
Curtis, James
Curtis, John

D

Daley, Charles
Daugherty, Nancy
Davison, Josiah
Davis, James
Davis, Robert
Davis, Samuel
Davis, Thomas
Davison, Andrew
Davison, Josiah
Davisson, John
Davos, John
Deshai, John
Devore, Jeremiah
Devore, Nikolas
Dill, Solomon
Disher, Christopher

Dixon, William
Doniphen, Anderson
Doniphen, Joseph
Donivan, Ephream
Donivan, Joseph
Dowden, John
Downing, Ellis
Downing, John
Downing, Robert
Downing, Timothy
Downing, Timothy, Jr.
Drake, Philip
Duvall, P. John
Dye, John
Dye, Stephen

E

Eaglebrier, Martin
Eales, John
Earl, David

Edwards, James
Edwards, James, Jr.
Ellis, John

F

Feagins, Daniel
Feagins, Fielding
Fee, John
Fee, Thomas
Fee, Thomas, Jr.
Fee, William
Ferree, John
Fields, Simon
Fields, Suth.
Fink, Daniel
Fisher, George
Fitzgerald, Benjamine

Fitzgerald, William
Forbes, William
Foster, Nathaniel
Fowler, Edward
Fowler, Edward, Jr.
Fowler, James
Frakes, Robert
Frakes, William
Frasure, Benjamine
Furmon, Thomas
Furr, Edwin

G

Gale, John
Galoway, John
Gardner, Abraham
Gash, Thomas
Gaskins, John
Gates, William
Gennings, William
Gill, Edward
Goble, Calib

Goble, Daniel
Goforth, William
Goodey, William
Gormon, William
Gragson, Richard
Green, Leonard
Gunsaulas, Daniel
Gunsaulas, James

H

Hambletun, Alexander
Hansaker, Jacob
Hardin, John
Hardister, Uriah
Harison, John
Harper, William
Hary, Charles
Hatfield, Adam
Hathaway, Silas
Hathaway, William
Haynes, Thomas
Headley, George
Heazelton, Daniel
Hellmun, Joseph

Helms, Meridith
Helms, William
Henderson, Andrew
Henry, John
Hester, Martin
Hook, John
Hough, John
Howel, Abner
Hughey, Alexander
Hughey, Charles
Hughey, Jane
Hughey, John
Hunter, Patrick

I

Irland, Hance

Irland, James

J

Jackman, Edward
Jackson, Mary
Johns, John
Johnston, John
Johnston, Thomas
Johnston, William

Jolley, Alexander
Jones, Jacob
Jones, Michael
Jones, William
Judd, Daniel
Jurdin, Samuel

K

Kelley, Joseph
Kelly, John
Kelly, Nathan
Kelsey, James
Kelsey, Thomas
Kelsey, Thomas, Jr.

Kenton, John
Kenton, Simon
Kiger, George
Kiger, John
Kilgore, Samuel
King, John

L

Lake, Asa
Lakin, Benjamine
Lakin, Joseph
Lakin, Samuel
Laney, John
Legate, Alexander
Leitch, David
Leonard, Jese
Leonard, Valentine
Levingston, David
Lewis, John

Light, Jacob
Lindsey, Thomas
Logan, John
Logan, Samuel
Logan, William
Lounsdale, Thomas
Love, Leonard
Loyd, D. Richard
Lucas, Abraham
Lunt, Ezra
Lyne, James

M

Machis, John
Mains, George
Markland, Jonathan
Marsh, William
Marshall, James
Marshall, Richard
Marshall, Thomas, Jr.

Marshell, Robert
Masters, Richard
Masterson, John
McArthur, John
McCan, Lanty
McClure, James
McCormack, James

M—Continued

McCullock, Joseph
McDonald, Joseph
McDonald, Valintine
McFarland, Samuel
McGinness, Thomas
McGunkins, William
McKindley, James
McKindley, Richard
McKinsey, Mordica
McMicheal, Margit
McNight, John
McNulley, Hugh
Mears, David
Meek, Robert
Melott, Thomas
Meranda, Isack
Meranda, James
Meranda, James, Jr.

Meranda, Samuel
Merrill, Joseph
Merrill, Reuben
Miles, James
Miller, James
Miller, John
Miller, John, Jr.
Miller, Robert
Mills, Elijah
Mills, Jacob
Mitcheal, Samuel
Mofford, Daniel
More, William
Morow, James
Moulton, Lerry
Murphey, David
Murphey, Deniss
Murphy, James

N

Nailer, Samuel
Newlin, George
Newlin, Harrod

Newman, Elias
Nicholas, Thomas

O

Oliver, John
Osburn, Ebenezer
Osburn, Morice

Overfield, Abner
Owins, Wm.

P

Patten, John
Peck, Daniel
Peddicord, John
Penner, John

Perry, Samuel
Pickett, William
Pribles, James
Price, Pugh

"AN OLD TIME MOUNTAIN HOME"

Two-story weatherboarded frame houses with porches upstairs and down typified the best architecture of the Big Sandy Valley from 1825 to 1850. Such homes were not only very comfortable but were surrounded by every good cheer.

R

Rains, John
Rains, William
Ralison, Richard
Ramsey, Hanah
Rankins, Moses
Rankins, Robert
Rardin, Ann
Rardon, Timothy
Ratleif, William
Records, Laban
Recter, Frederick
Reddick, Thomas
Redick, Joseph
Redin, Reubin
Redmun, Daniel
Redmun, Gabriel
Reed, Jacob
Reed, John
Reed, William
Rees, Thomas
Reval, Adam
Reves, Austin

Reves, Benjamine
Reynolds, Jonah
Riccords, Josiah
Riccords, Spencer
Richards, Daniel
Riddle, Isack
Riffle, Jacob
Right, Robert
Ringland, James
Riordin, John
Rippy, Henrey
Ritchey, David
Ritchey, William
Robison, William
Rogers, Henrey
Rose, Enoch
Rose, Jonathan
Ross, Jonathan
Ross, Richard
Rubart, John
Ruth, Davis
Ryan, Micheal

S

Sallars, Elizabeth
Scott, John
Scott, John
Sellers, John
Sellers, Leonard
Sergent, Thomas
Shannon, Jeremiah
Shaw, James
Shawhan, Derbey
Slow, Thomas
Smith, Alexander
Smith, Andrew
Smith, David
Smith, Jese
Smith, Samuel
Smith, William
Smock, Mathew
South, William

Spencer, John
Spencer, William
Sroufe, Adam
Sroufe, Boston
Steers, Hugh
Stephenson, John
Stephenson, Joseph
Stephenson, Nathan
Stephenson, Richard
Stephenson, Thomas
Stephenson, William
Stillwill, Joseph
Stoutt, Hosea
Stoutt, Job
Stuart, William
Sutters, George
Swan, Hugh

T

Tatman, James
Tatman, Joseph
Taylor, Henry
Taylor, James, Jr.
Taylor, James, Sr.
Taylor, John, Jr.
Taylor, John, Sr.
Taylor, Robert
Taylor, Simon
Teel, William
Tenniss, Samuel
Tharp, Andrew
Thomas, Absalum
Thomas, Philomon

Thomas, William
Thompson, Bennerd
Thompson, Mary
Thompson, Mathew
Thompson, Price
Tigart, Arthur
Tingley, Levi
Tout, Abraham
Travis, Nickodemus
Treacle, Stephen
Trushell, Solomon
Tuel, Barton
Turner, James

V

Vansickle, William

Vaughan, Daniel

W

Walker, David
Walker, Obedian
Walker, William
Ward, Charles
Washburn, Cornelious
Washburn, Jeremiah
Washburn, Joseph
Waters, Josephus
Watson, Robert
Waugh, John
Weathringtun, John
Weathringtun, Joseph
Weathringtun, William
Welch, Anthoney
Welch, Christopher
Wells, Nathan
Wells, Robert
West, James
West, John
Westbrook, Richard
Whaley, John
White, David

White, Francis
White, Levy
White, Stephen
White, Thomas
Wiley, Elisha
Wiley, John
Wiley, Robert
Wiley, Water
Williams, Thomas
Wills, James
Winn, John
Woocutt, John
Wood, Amey
Wood, Benjamine
Wood, Christopher
Wood, George
Wood, William
Woodard, William
Woods, Jeremiah
Woods, Thomas
Woods, Tobias
Wright, Joseph

Y

York, Charles
Young, John

Youngman, Jacob
Youngman, Jacob, Jr.

THE LOWER SETTLEMENTS

While the settlements of the upper Big Sandy progressed through migrations from the New, the Clinch and Holston valleys, the continued hostility of the Shawnees in the Ohio Valley made it impossible for the settlers to gain a foothold in the lower part of the Big Sandy. In 1793, travelers passing down the Ohio to central Kentucky found no inhabitants at the mouth of the Big Sandy.[12] The town sites of Catlettsburg and Ashland were then a primeval wilderness, and gave no indication of the large settlement that was taking place in the upper part of the Big Sandy Valley. As late as 1796 and 1797 the banks of the Ohio from Pittsburgh to Maysville were almost uninhabited. It is said that at this time there were scarcely thirty families scattered along this great stretch of over 400 miles of inland waterway. Following conclusions of peace with the Indians in 1795, however, emigration became rapid, and by 1802 log cabins of the settlers were dotted all along the banks of the Ohio, and were frequently in sight of each other.[13]

Finally, though not until about 1807, the strategic position of Catlettsburg—at the mouth of the Big Sandy—was seen. About that time two large houses, one of logs and the other clapboarded with a sign post before the door, stood at this point, and marked the future location of the city. One good brick house also stood at the mouth of Keys Creek on the Ohio, now known as Normal. A little farther on a gentleman by the name of A. M. Colvin had an excellent frame house on the Kentucky shore opposite Hanging Rock. This was near the site of Ashland.[14] Judge Jesse Bryan Boone— son of Daniel Boone, the pioneer, who lived here[15] with his son for a time following the establishment of the county in 1804—was then justice of the peace in Greenup County, Kentucky, and undoubtedly exercised some authority well up into the Big Sandy Valley, because of the remoteness of Prestonsburg, the seat of Floyd County.

Though the first quarter of the nineteenth century witnessed the settling of the lower Big Sandy Valley with great rapidity, a large portion of the people who came in were nothing more than squatters who occupied without question land which had been surveyed and was owned by others. Early travelers going by boat down the Ohio River frequently spent the night at the settlement at the mouth of the Big

Sandy, and thus became acquainted with the existing conditions. Thomas Nuttall, a cultured gentleman of Philadelphia, who in his overland journey to the great southwest spent the night of November 7, 1818, with some settlers near the mouth of the Big Sandy, wrote as follows in his Journal[16] concerning his impression of the people and the region:

"Near to this line (Eastern boundary of Kentucky) commences the first appearance of the cane (Arundinaria macrosperma), which seems to indicate some difference in the climate and soil. The settlements are here remote, the people poor, and along the river not so characteristically hospitable as in the interior of Kentucky. Landing rather late, we took up our lodging where there happened to be a corn-husking, and were kept awake with idle merriment and riot till past midnight. Some of the party, or rather of the two national parties, got up and harangued to a judge, like so many lawyers, on some political argument, and other topics, in a boisterous and illiberal style, but without coming to blows.

"The cornfields at this season of the year, are so overrun with cuckold-burs (Xanthium strumarium), and the seeds of different species of Bidens or Spanish-needles, (30) as to prove extremely troublesome to woolen clothes, and to the domestic cattle, which are loaded with them in tormenting abundance. In consequence of these weeds, the fleece of the sheep is scarcely worth the trouble of shearing.

"The people here, living upon exigencies, and given to rambling about instead of attending to their farms, are very poor and uncomfortable in every respect; but few of them possess the land on which they live. Having spent everything in unsuccessful migration, and voluntarily exiling themselves from their connections in society, they begin to discover, when too late, that industry would have afforded that comfort and independence which they in vain seek in the solitudes of an unhealthy wilderness. We found it almost impossible to purchase any kind of provisions, even butter or bacon, nothing appearing to be cultivated scarcely but corn and a little wheat. I was again informed of the existence of aboriginal remains in the vicinity of the place where we arrived this evening."

But the abject conditions so clearly portrayed by Nuttall as existing among the people close about the mouth of Big Sandy did not extend far up the river. It must be remembered that the Ohio River was at this early time the great inland highway of immigration to the west and southwest. Down it came many classes of people, desirable and undesirable. Those with little or no substance stayed close to the main river, rarely venturing up the larger tributaries, such as the Kanawha and Big Sandy, except for very short distances. Their habitations, miserable for the most part, were generally of a temporary nature, in which they eked out an existence based on very slight and intermittent effort. It may be pointed out that even to this day the Ohio River is infested with a similar class of people who, drifting along with the current in houseboats and flatboats of every description, neither work nor worry beyond the bare necessities of life, which an indulgent society accords them as a matter of custom.

The Immigrant Trail

The settlement of the upper Big Sandy was in fact an overflow from the great stream of immigration westward bound from the seaboard towns in Pennsylvania, New York, New Jersey, Maryland, and the plantations of Virginia and the Carolinas. These people were for the most part home-seekers and adventurers, rough and ready to a degree, but slightly understood

to-day. Native intelligence, ability and good
health made up for a general deficiency in
advanced education, which indeed would have
found little opportunity for practical use during this early period. Making their way up
the great valley of Virginia, with the Blue
Ridge to the east and the Alleghenys on the
west, the most of these pioneers passed from
the Shenandoah onto the headwaters of the
New River, and thence to the Holston, the
Clinch and the Powell rivers.

From this point the principal trail lead most
of them through the Cumberland Gap into central Kentucky over the Wilderness Road.
Some keeping on, however, followed down the
Clinch and Holston and made their way overland into central Tennessee, while others
continued to push even farther into the southwest. During the height of this great trans-
monstane migration from 1785 to 1810, a few
annually turned northward into the New River
Valley, and others left the trail for the north
at Fort Chiswell. These were principally
Virginians and Carolinians who were attracted
by the reports of the rich bottoms in the Big
Sandy Valley. They made their way over the
heads of the Tug and the Levisa Forks, some
coming over Pound Gap. All were prepared to

THE POUND GAP TRAIL

Over this "trace," each in turn, passed the buffalo, the Indian, the explorer, and the homesteader of the **Big Sandy Valley**.

resist the hostility of the roving Shawnees and Cherokees who still infested this region. By so doing they hoped to prove their title to the desired land, and re-establish in this western wilderness the system of plantations so richly productive in the river valleys east of the mountains.

Isaac Weld, an educated young gentleman from Dublin, Ireland, in commenting later on his experience along the Wilderness Trail in Virginia during the years 1795-1797 said:[17]

"As I passed along the road from Fincastle to the Potowmak which is the high road from the Northern States to Kentucky, I met with great numbers of people from Kentucky and the new State of Tennessee going towards Philadelphia and Baltimore, and with many others going in a contrary direction to 'explore,' as they call it, that is to search for lands conveniently situated for new settlements in the western country. These people all travel on horseback, with pistols or swords, and a large blanket folded up under their saddle. There are now houses scattered along nearly the whole way from Fincastle to Lexington, in Kentucky. It would be still dangerous for any person to venture singly; but if five or six travel together they are perfectly secure. Formerly travelers were always obliged to go forty or fifty in a party.''

It was indeed a time and a place for stout hearts. Only the hardiest and most adventuresome of this great westward moving cavalcade dared to leave the beaten trail to attempt the possession of the choice lands on the headwaters of the Big Sandy. A naturally selective process, it early determined the fibre of the men and women who were to settle the upper part of the valley. And later this strength of character and physical prowess which had been the necessary asset of the pioneers became the heritage for one of the most notable groups of families of any part of the southern Appalachians.

POPULATION GROWTH

The unique story of the settlement of the Big Sandy Valley, thus told chronologically by incident and tradition, is enriched somewhat by an examination of the figures of growth of the regional population. In the way of resumé it is seen that in 1790 the trans-Allegheny settlements were principally confined to central Kentucky centering about Lexington and Louisville, and to central Tennessee centering about

Nashville. There was also a small settlement on the Ohio near the mouth of the Kanawha River. The Big Sandy Valley lying between was virtually an unpeopled wilderness still traversed by vicious Indian bands and an occasional hunter-pioneer. Ten years later in 1800 a few outlying cabins or "stations" were located in the lower and upper parts of the valley. In 1810 while the extreme headwaters of the Levisa Fork were still unsettled, a population of from two to six persons to the square mile was resident in the lower part of the valley. At the same time a restricted portion of central Kentucky and eastern Tennessee many miles to the west showed from forty-five to ninety persons to the square mile.

At the end of the next decade, in 1820, the Big Sandy Valley was virtually all taken up by homesteaders or speculators, but the population did not average as much as six inhabitants to the square mile. During the next twenty years the growth of population was greatest in the lower part of the valley, where in 1840[18] it ranged from six to eighteen persons to the square mile. The reason for the change is found in the gradual opening up of the Ohio as the main route of travel to the Southwest, and the virtual abandonment of the old overland road—the Wilderness Trail. The head of the Big Sandy Valley continued to slowly increase in population, but the growth was largely that of the native born, while in the lower part of the valley the natural increase in the population was greatly augmented by the persistent homesteaders from the North.

NOTES TO CHAPTER IV

[1] Calendar Virginia State Papers, Vol. I, p. 265. Also First Report of Department Archives and History of West Virginia. V. A. Lewis, Vol. I, p. 111.

[2] Kentucky Land Grant Book 14, p. 266. John Rogers patent. Land Office, Frankfort, Kentucky.

[3] Hanson's Journal in Documentary History of Dunmore's War. Thwaites-Kellogg, pp. 11-133.

[4] Revolution on the Upper Ohio. Thwaites-Kellogg, pp. 13-14.

[5] Founding of Harman's Station. Connelley, pp. 27-35.

[6] Founding of Harman's Station. Connelley, pp. 68-69.

[7] Memoranda of the Preston Family, by John Mason Brown, pp. 1-31.

[8] Map of the State of Kentucky. Imlay, 1793.

[9] Barker's Map of Kentucky, 1795. Also Early Western Travels. Thwaites, Vol. III. French Map, "Des Estate Unis," 1804. Opposite p. 109.

[10] The Big Sandy Valley. Ely, pp. 11 and 12.

[11] (Original) Tax List for District No. 1 (Floyd County) of Mason County (1793), Archives Kentucky State Historical Society.

[12] Travels into Kentucky, Michaux, in Early Western Travels. Thwaites, Vol. III, p. 35.

[13] A Tour to the Western Country, Cuming, in Early Western Travels. Thwaites, Vol. IV, pp. 154-156.

[14] A Tour to the Western Country, Cuming, in Early Western Travels. Thwaites, Vol. IV, pp. 154-156.

[15] The Register, Kentucky State Historical Society, Vol. VI, No. 18, p. 102 (1908).

[16] Travels into the Arkansas Territory, Nuttall, in Early Western Travels. Thwaites, Vol. XIII, pp. 58-59.

[17] Travels in Virginia in Revolutionary Times. Edited by A. J. Morrison, Lynchburg, Virginia, 1922, pp. 108-109.

[18] United States Census Reports, 1790 to 1840.

CHAPTER V

RELIGIOUS DEVELOPMENT

Pioneers in every sense of the word, and profoundly religious, it was many years before the settlers of the Big Sandy Valley began the erection of their first church houses. Indeed, the first serious concern of these hardy people was to get enough dwelling houses—generally built of logs rough-hewn from the forest—to satisfy the growing demands of a rapidly increasing body of immigrants. Fortunately, a fine, old custom of the land and the time made churches something else than an absolute necessity. Every dwelling was in a sense a church, where daily prayers were said. Frequently large gatherings were held, either inside these residences during the inclement weather or outside in shady groves along the creeks or rivers when the elements were propitious. The first inhabitants of the Big Sandy Valley region were almost without exception Methodists, Baptists, and Presbyterians. Other denominations were scarcely represented.

THE EARLY METHODISTS

The Big Sandy River Circuit makes its first appearance in the Minutes of the Methodist

Church in 1809 when it is noted that the
Rev. Benjamin Edge is appointed to this
district, with James Ward, who was a middle-
aged man, presiding Elder. Cornelius McGuire,
a local preacher, having preceded the Rev. Edge
by a decade or more, was the first to introduce
Methodism in the Big Sandy Valley. He came
from Tazewell County, Virginia, with the first
settlers prior to the beginning of the nineteenth
century, and in company with seventy-five
others settled on the Big Sandy River in that
region which extends from where Pikeville now
stands to the mouth of Johns Creek, a distance
of thirty-five miles. The records show that the
first Methodist Society was organized by
Mr. McGuire at the house of Henry Stratton in
1796, and consisted of Cornelius McGuire and
wife, William J. Mays and wife, Henry Stratton and wife, a number of the Laynes, Johns,
Auxiers, and others.[1]

It was about the time of the War of 1812
that the Big Sandy Circuit was established in
the Southern province of the Methodist Church.
One of the first ordained preachers to ride this
circuit was Rev. Marcus Lindsay, who was a
divine of talent and culture. He made a lasting
impression throughout the region. Following
him, about 1834, the Rev. William B. Landrum

took up his duties among the people of this rough and sparsely settled country. In these early days Bishop Hubbard H. Kavanaugh preached many times in the lower part of the Big Sandy Valley. Other local preachers were Rev. R. D. Callihan, Methodist, who lived in Ashland; the Rev. James Pelphrey, Baptist, Johnston County; and the Rev. Wallace Bailey, Baptist, Magoffin County. All were notable preachers during the first half of the nineteenth century. The Rev. John Borders, Benjamin P. Porter, Andrew Johnson, George W. Price, and Goodwin Lycans, all Baptists, began their noteworthy backwoods service toward the close of the period covered by this history. Besides these preachers who lived in or rode the Big Sandy Circuit, there were a number of others, notably Burwell and Stephen Spurlock, who lived on Twelvepole Creek in Virginia, and the Rev. Philip Strother, a native of Carter County, Kentucky, who frequently came into the Big Sandy district to hold their preachings.[2]

It is said that one of the most eccentric of the early Baptist preachers was the Rev. Henry Dixon, who was quite as good a fiddler as a preacher. It was no uncommon thing to see him with his fiddle under his arm on his way to church. The fact that he always opened and closed his services with his own music in a country where music of any kind was indeed scarce, made him unusually popular. The life of the preacher riding the Big Sandy Circuit in the early days was an exacting one. For his outfit he had a good horse, saddle, bridle, a comfortable suit of clothes and a warm overcoat. Usually he was equipped with a pair of saddle-bags, in one of which he carried such changes of clothing as he needed, and in the other a small Bible and hymn-book. He lived with the people to whom he ministered, and was one of them in every way. His journeys, always lonely and fatiguing, took him through wild and unsettled regions. He stayed wherever night or storm overtook him, and no cabin was too small or poor to show him welcome and hospitality.

REV. KAVANAUGH ON BIG SANDY

For many years the Little Sandy and Big Sandy Circuits were combined, and when the Rev. Kavanaugh, later Bishop Kavanaugh, first rode through this rugged and unsettled district, there were no established roads or other lines of communication. Nothing that could really be called a road existed between Lexington and Maysville or between the mouth of Big Sandy

A HOUSEHOLD DUTY

Spinning yarn on the porches was a practice enforced by necessity from the earliest times.
Many hand-made coverlets upward of a hundred years old are still to be found in the Big Sandy Valley.

and the settlements farther up the river. Trails and bridle paths only were to be found along the streams and rivers. The Sandy Circuit was large. It extended from the mouth of the Big Sandy River south to the headwaters in Pike County, and covered all the territory which is now included in Greenup, Lawrence, Boyd, Carter, Elliott, Morgan, Johnson, Martin, Floyd, Knott, and Pike counties. There were twenty-four preaching places, and each place had to be filled at least every four weeks. The work was divided between Bishop Kavanaugh and the Rev. Luke P. Allen, who was the senior preacher of the region.

It is interesting to note that no preacher of this early period considered his equipment complete without a small marking iron. This tool consisted of a sharp pointed iron rod about six inches long, and was used to mark a tree, generally a beech, at the fork of the road, so that there would be no difficulty in finding the route thereafter. This method of tree marking was in the nature of blazing, except that it was not done with a hatchet. It is amusing to learn that in many instances these godly men, preoccupied with their thoughts, either forgot to do their marking and so became lost, or marked their trees incorrectly, and thereby frequently confused themselves. There is many an incident on record where the preachers were entirely thrown off their regular route, or else were forced to double back on themselves, because of their failure to mark the trees correctly.

About the time that Mr. McGuire was engaged in completing the organization of the Methodist Society in the vicinity of lower Johns Creek, Mr. William Buchanan, a native of Pennsylvania, moved to the Big Sandy Valley and settled on the Kentucky side about sixteen miles above the mouth of the river. Buchanan post office still marks the locality. He was a Presbyterian and one of the earliest of this denomination in the section. The Rev. John Johnson succeeded the Rev. Edge in this district and organized a Methodist Society in the northern part of the Valley, where a church was built on a lot donated by Buchanan in 1846. Shortly thereafter another Society was formed at the house of Charles Riggs, one mile above the mouth of Big Sandy, close to the river bank, on land later owned by Rev. William Hampton. From 1813 to 1836 the dwelling of Mr. Riggs was used as a regular chapel. Subsequently the home of Rev. Hampton was used.

About the middle of the century a church was built jointly by the Methodists and Presbyterians.

In 1812 a Methodist Society was formed at John Burgess's, eight miles above Louisa. About the same time another was organized at the mouth of Paint Creek in the house which was later occupied by Moses Preston. Preaching was also held in the homes of Hezekiah Borders and Judge Borders. The Prestonsburg Methodist Society which was organized about this time was generally held at the home of Harry B. Mayo, and later at the home of Lewis Mayo. Soon thereafter a Society of Methodists was organized at Pikeville, and then at adjacent points along the river under the direction of ordained itinerant preachers, chief among whom was the Rev. Kavanaugh.[3]

BAPTIST SOCIETIES AND CUSTOMS

Although the Methodists were undoubtedly the first to effect a permanent organization in the Big Sandy Valley, they were but slightly in advance of those settlers professing the Baptist faith. The United Baptists, as they were called, were composed of a large Association of local Societies: which were known as the Union, Big Blain, Paint Union, Open Fork of Paint

Creek, George's Creek, Rockcastle, Silver
Creek, Little Blain, Toms Creek, Prestonsburg,
Zion, Hoods Fork, Mates Creek, and Burning
Springs churches. Many of these infant Baptist
Societies were formed very early in the nineteenth century. In this association of churches,
the Rev. John Borders was one of the most
active and able preachers. The Rev. William
Wells, Cornwallis Bailey, James Pelphrey,[4]
and James Williamson, who served from 1825
until after the middle of the nineteenth century,
were co-laborers with the Rev. Borders.

These hardy preachers of a day now all but
forgotten were strong-minded, picturesque
characters. Their whole-souled, practical re-
ligion was thoroughly in keeping with the times
and the region, and their visits were regarded
as a treat, breaking the social monotony and
isolation of log cabin life. To the pioneer, the
circuit rider was the personification of faith,
integrity, endurance and frugality. These self-
evident traits, so much admired by all people,
were brought out in the early preachers by the
Big Sandy Circuit itself. The precipitous cliffs,
the natural cane-brake, the flooded stream, the
uncharted forest, the beasts of prey and the
occasional stalking savage, all made for strength
of character. Preacher and parishioner faring
alike developed a strong unity of feeling.

The clothing of the settler for the most part was taken from the gray and red buck that roamed the hills. Articles of "home spun" were added to these, and gradually became more common. The bread, baked in an open fire, was simply made from corn meal, which had been beaten in a mortar by hand. The meat of the times was bear, venison, turkey, and squirrel. To these were added wild honey, tree or maple sugar, sorghum, and berries. Many of the settlers made their own liquor, which stood for the times as well as hospitality. Intemperance, however, was uncommon, and disorderly conduct almost unknown.

The early Baptists of the Big Sandy Valley, as elsewhere in the State, were distinguished by the titles Regular and Separate. The Separate Baptists were more extreme Calvinists than the Regular Baptists. They refused to adopt any creed or confession of faith, and were constantly changing in their doctrinal views. Although the Regular and Separate Baptists of Virginia and North Carolina finally adopted the Philadelphia Confession of Faith almost unanimously, thereby paving a way for an easy union between them, this did not occur in Kentucky. The freedom of many of the Baptists of early times may be seen in a number of primitive customs which prevailed among them. Some of these were taken from other religious societies, and some were necessarily expedients of the times, which have since been improved upon or eliminated. The ceremony of "laying on of hands" was in common use among the early Baptists of Virginia and Kentucky, including the Big Sandy Valley. Probably several centuries old, it was logically the equivalent of extending the right hand of fellowship to persons after baptism, and has long since been discontinued. "The washing of the feet,"[5] still spoken of as "Feet Washing," was a common ceremony among the early Baptists of the Big Sandy Valley. The custom still persists. It prevailed to some extent among the Regular Baptists, but was practically a part of the ceremony among the Separate Baptists. In these early days, quarterly meetings were frequently held during the summer months, at which times all of the members of a certain group of churches would congregate at one place to enjoy an extended preaching. Besides affording a wide expression of religious feeling at a time when the Big Sandy Valley was but sparsely settled, these quarterly meetings formed a real and much needed social diversion for the young folks as well as their elders.

MAKING HAND ''GRITS.''

The task of ''grittin'' corn usually fell to the small boy or girl. Women used spinning wheels like that on the left, while the old men ground the corn in the hand mills like that on the right.

Within the Presbyterian church organization, the Synod of Virginia, listed, among others, the Presbytery of Transylvania. This backwoods province included the adjacent regions of eastern Tennessee, southwestern Virginia and the Big Sandy Valley. Though there were a few scattered Presbyterians in eastern Kentucky early in the nineteenth century, they were unable to form well organized churches. It was for this reason that the growth and expansion of the Presbyterian organization in the Big Sandy Valley region came many years after that of the Methodist and Baptist churches.[6]

NOTES TO CHAPTER V

[1] History of Methodism in Kentucky. Redford. 1870. Vol. III, pp. 404, 440.

[2] The Big Sandy Valley. Ely, p. 24.

[3] Life and Times of Rev. H. H. Kavanaugh. Redford.

[4] History of Kentucky Baptists. Vol. II. C. H. Spencer, pp. 509-513.

[5] History of Kentucky Baptists. Vol. I. C. H. Spencer, p. 486.

[6] History of the Presbyterian Church in the State of Kentucky. Davidson, p. 81.

CHAPTER VI

SOCIAL AND ECONOMIC EXPANSION

(1800 to 1850)

There is perhaps no other region in Kentucky which was as rapidly settled and as soon divided into county units for local self-government as the Big Sandy Valley. The reason for this is seen in the fact that the territory was from a topographic standpoint a veritable cul-de-sac which was easily held by the Indians long after they ceased to exercise control over adjacent regions. Years before the white man could enter the Big Sandy with security, the Bluegrass region to the west and southwest, as well as the mountainous districts to the east, were fairly developed. General Anthony Wayne's decisive stroke at Fallen Timbers in 1795, however, left the Indians broken and humiliated and caused them to withdraw permanently from the Big Sandy Valley, thereby throwing open for immediate settlement the last territory in which large tracts of excellent land close to the east could be procured for the taking.

The Boundary of Floyd County

At the date of its formation, in 1799, Floyd County[1] comprised the whole Big Sandy Valley and some adjacent area. It was the fortieth county created in Kentucky, and was named after Colonel John Floyd, the daring Indian fighter and surveyor.[2] The boundary lines of Floyd County when first established were vague and uncertain both on paper and in the field. The eastern and southeastern limits coincided with that of Kentucky and Virginia, and hence involved questions which were greatly in dispute between the two States. These lines had never been surveyed with accuracy. Kentucky County, from which the State took its boundary, was considered to have the same territorial limitations as had been ascribed to western Virginia prior to the separation. The new State was generally regarded as lying west of the crest of the Cumberland Mountains and the Big Sandy River, but the exact location of the dividing ridges was unknown.

To eliminate border arguments which naturally grew out of this territorial uncertainty, the Kentucky Legislature in 1795 passed an act authorizing the Governor to take up the matter with the Governor of Virginia. This was done, and in due course each State appointed three commissioners clothed with authority to interpret the existing laws by settling the growing controversy by definitely locating the line. Difficulties of a large nature arose in the course of the deliberations of the joint commission which served to delay the final decision for several years.

At last a joint meeting was held at the forks of the Big Sandy in October, 1799.[3] There is an interesting tradition concerning the manner in which the Tug Fork was selected, thereby giving to Kentucky the greater part of the territory drained by the Levisa Fork and a part of that drained by the Tug Fork. It is said that the commissioners arrived at the point where Louisa now stands late in the day. Autumnal rains had been falling in the valley and both forks of the Big Sandy were rising. During the course of the evening it was decided that the boundary line should follow the largest fork of the Big Sandy. Throughout the night the Tug Fork rose steadily and in the morning it appeared to be a much larger stream than the Levisa Fork. The commissioners who were no doubt in a much better position to pass on the genial hospitality and appetizing refreshments

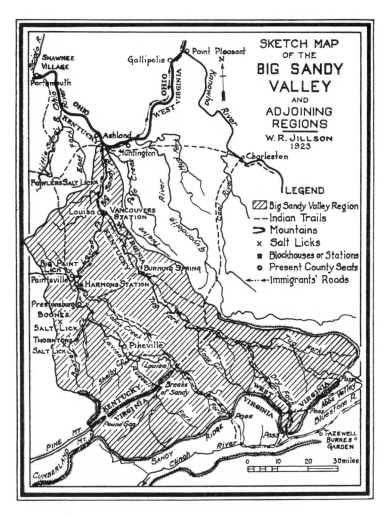

MAP OF THE BIG SANDY VALLEY

The overland pioneers came up the Bluestone trail, and crossing over the divide, passed down the Tug, the Dry or Levisa Forks. Many went in over the Pound Gap from the Clinch River trails. Others came by boat down the Ohio and up the Sandy River to the neighborhood of Louisa.

of the pioneers of the valley, than they were on the size of the competing water sheds, decided that the Kentucky-Virginia boundary should lie in the waters of the Tug Fork.

What delightful conviviality followed this august determination is an open speculation, but it is known that the commissioners departed before the slow rising tide of the Levisa River reached the forks, and all too plainly told which was the largest fork of the Big Sandy River. Widespread good humor resulted when it was learned that the smaller of the two—the Tug Fork—was chosen as the Virginia boundary. Mountain land was the cheapest and most easily secured of all things at that time, and it was not until years afterward, when a part of Lawrence, all of Martin and the greater portions of Johnson, Floyd, and Pike counties were carved out of the territory so fortunately gained for Kentucky, that the real importance of the boundary decision became apparent. Had the decision been otherwise, the train of subsequent events must needs have been much altered and with it this history, for the greater part of the Big Sandy Valley would have remained a part of Virginia.

Division of Floyd County

This vast territory was later broken up into several counties, the largest of which is Pike, formed in 1821 out of part of Floyd and named for General Zebulon Pike.[4] Piketon at the juncture of the Levisa and Russell forks of the Big Sandy was the first county seat. Tradition has it that one of the early Pike county courts was also held in a private dwelling at the mouth of Shelby Creek. The earliest Pike County record (App. F.) says that the first court was held at the house of Spencer Adkins on Monday, March 4, 1822. Simeon Justice, James Roberts, Reuben Retherford, John Hunt and John Bevins were constituted the first justices of Pike County under appointment and seal of Governor John Adair. These locations were abandoned in 1825 and the present town of Pikeville was made the county seat.

Lawrence County[5] was erected out of parts of Greenup and Floyd in 1821, the sixty-ninth in order of formation. Louisa was made the county seat. It was at this little town at the forks of the Big Sandy that the westward currents of immigration from the north and the south met. The New England and Pennsylvanian pioneers came down the Ohio and up the Big Sandy, the Virginian and Carolinian settlers came over the mountains and down the Big Sandy. Louisa soon reflected a composite culture which was to stimulate its growth and last for many a generation. Lawrence County was named after Captain James Lawrence of the United States Navy, who in 1803 took such an important part in our Mediterranean engagements with the Tripoli pirates. As originally created, the county embraced what is now Lawrence County and certain other adjacent territories which later became parts of Boyd, Carter, Elliott, Morgan, Johnson, and Martin counties. The act designated as commissioners to select the site of a "permanent seat of justice" for the new county, John Rice, James Ward, Jr., Henry B. Mayo, Samuel May and David K. Harris. These commissioners having chosen the lands at the forks of the Big Sandy, where Louisa now stands, the Kentucky General Assembly established Louisa as the official county seat by an act effective December 11, 1922. The first trustees were Samuel Bell, Andrew Johnson, Isaac Bolt, Nimrod Canterberry, Andrew Chapman, Joseph R. Ward and Elisha Welmond.[6]

In 1843 Johnson County was formed with its county seat at Paintsville, which had been an old trading-post called Paint Lick Station. It was the ninety-seventh county organized in Kentucky and was named in honor of Col. Richard M. Johnson. Parts of Floyd, Lawrence, and Morgan counties were assembled to produce Johnson County, which embraces within its territory the old Shawnee Village on Mudlick Creek. Many interesting Indian traditions cling to this part of the Big Sandy Valley. The earliest county record obtainable at Paintsville says: "At a Court held for the County of Johnson at the court house in the Town of Paintsville on the 3d day of June 1844, Present—Shadrick Preston, Elcana Howes, Constantine Conley, John Stafford and Frances A. Brown."

Boyd County was formed in 1860 out of parts of Greenup, Carter and Lawrence, with Catlettsburg as the county seat. It was the one hundred and seventh county and was named for former Lieutenant Governor Linn Boyd. Ten years later, in 1870, Martin County was organized from parts of Johnson, Pike and Floyd. It was named for Colonel John P. Martin, a distinguished and cultured gentleman of Prestonsburg. The county seat of Martin was originally known as Eden, but was later changed to Inez.

Previous to 1779 the lower Big Sandy Valley had been a part of Mason County, which, having been formed in 1788,[7] was the easternmost part of the State when Kentucky was admitted into the Union in 1792.[8] At an earlier date this region was a part of Fincastle County, and later Kentucky County, Virginia. The latter county, destined soon to become the fifteenth State in the Union, was separated from Fincastle County by legislative action in December, 1776.

In Virginia, Buchanan, Dickenson and the northeastern portion of Wise counties constitute the headwaters of the Levisa, Russell and Pound forks of the Big Sandy River. In West Virginia, all of McDowell and the western parts of Mingo and Wayne counties are included within the Tug Fork basin. The first Mingo County Court was organized February 7, 1895, at Williamson, which was selected as the county seat. J. K. Anderson, James L. Deskins, and Alex Stafford were the Commissioners. Buchanan County, Virginia, was formed from parts of Tazewell and Russell counties, Virginia, in 1858. The county seat, Grundy, has always been located at the junction of Slate Creek and the Levisa Fork of the Big Sandy. A courthouse fire during the year 1885 destroyed all the early records of Buchanan County. Dickenson County, Virginia, was erected from parts of Russell, Wise, and Buchanan counties, Virginia, in 1880. Its county seat is Clintwood on the Pound River.

Wise County, Virginia, was established in 1856, being made up of parts of Russell, Scott, and Lee counties. Its county seat is the town of Wise, situated on the divide between the Cranes' Nest River, a fork of the Pound River, and the Clinch River. Wise County, Virginia, records of Monday, July 28, 1856, show that there were present at the formation of the first court, William Richmond, William Roberson, William H. Dean, Nicholas Horne, Jessee Davis, Joseph Eastep, James Buckhanan, Isaac Willis, S. H. Senter, George H. Gray, Jeremiah Powers, Hiram Riggs, James Holbrook, James H. McCoy, Martin Kibern, John Creech, Daniel Short, John H. Vanover, Wm. Vanover, Charles E. Bond. Each of these men was formally commissioned a justice of the peace. On ballot, William Richmond was elected Presiding Justice of the first Wise County Court.

Wayne County, West Virginia, which includes a small portion of the lower part of the Big Sandy Valley adjoining the Ohio River, was formed from Cabell County in 1842 while

"WHIP SAWING" TIMBER.

All of the lumber used in the first "frame" houses of the Big Sandy region was produced by "whip saw" methods. It took real men to produce lumber after this fashion. Had it not been for the fact that labor was relatively cheap it would have been quite impractical.

a part of the "Old Dominion." The town of Wayne on Twelve Pole Creek was made the county seat. Both the county and the town were named in honor of General Anthony Wayne of Fallen Timbers fame. In 1894 Mingo County, West Virginia, which contains within its borders a small part of the Tug Fork of Big Sandy, was established by the division of Logan County. This county was named for the Mingo tribe of Indians. Williamson on the Tug Fork of the Big Sandy near the mouth of Pond Creek is the county seat.

EARLY LIVING CONDITIONS

The magnificent stand of broad-leafed timber throughout the Big Sandy Valley retarded for many years the agricultural development of the region. The settler found it necessary to clear his land before he could plant his crop. As early as 1807 cotton was more or less successfully raised along the Ohio River at the mouth of the Big Sandy Valley.[9] The principal crop, however, was corn, which on the deep, rich forest loam of this region was bountiful. Tobacco was raised for domestic purposes, as were many small grains and vegetables. During the early part of the nineteenth century a considerable export demand for ginseng root developed. Many settlers thus became during spare time "ginseng hunters," with the result that thousands of dollars were in this manner added to the total income of the Valley. The wealthier immigrants, including the Grahams, Morgans, Johns and a few other families, brought their slaves with them from the plantations in old Virginia and used them with varying success on the new farms in the Big Sandy bottom near Prestonsburg. Slavery flourished in the broad bottoms of the lower Big Sandy Valley and was instrumental in building up a considerable industry in tobacco.[10]

The virgin forests of the Big Sandy Valley were filled with all kinds of game during the first quarter of the nineteenth century. Bear existed in large numbers, and were killed by settlers who sold their hides to fur traders for a price which varied from $1.00 to $3.00.[11] These hides were held by the local dealers until a through trader bought them and flatboated them down the Big Sandy to the Ohio, thence up the river to Pittsburgh and to the northeast. Deer were plentiful throughout the country and wild turkey could be found at all points in the Valley, even to the mouth of the Big Sandy.[12] Both provided a staple and readily secured food for the settlers. Accounts were very commonly figured in English money as late as 1815, when one American dollar was worth six English shillings. School masters were employed privately by those who could afford them for their children. John Graham's account book shows that he employed one Thomas Lewis in 1812 at a salary of one English pound, sixteen shillings per month. This was at that time the equivalent of $6.50 and was to be taken out principally in bacon and wool with only six shillings in cash. Money was scarce, goods were plenty, and school teachers, unfortunately, not much in demand.

In the early days Limestone, which later was re-named Maysville, was the only town of importance near the Big Sandy. It served as a clearing house for Big Sandy trade much the same as Catlettsburg and Ashland do at present. This little river town in the early part of the nineteenth century was indeed a real port, for through it passed all travelers who had as a destination Lexington or central Kentucky.[13] Many Cincinnati, Louisville and far west sojourners also stopped there. About 1815, Joseph Ewing began store-keeping a quarter of a mile above the mouth of the Big Sandy River on the Virginia side,[14] but this small establishment, coupled with a house or two on the Kentucky side where Catlettsburg now stands, did not serve to hold much of the river trade. In 1815 Frederick Moore opened a store near the mouth of Big Sandy,[15] but many of the supplies needed by the settlers, especially in the upper part of the Valley, continued to be brought in on mule-back from Virginia over the headwaters of the Tug and Levisa forks, rather than down the Ohio and up the streams. About 1825, pole boating up the Big Sandy to bring supplies to the settlements near Prestonsburg and above, became a general practice. In 1837 a steamboat ascended the Big Sandy to Prestonsburg with importations from the East. The following day it took a pleasure party still farther up the river.[16]

MINERAL RESOURCES

The early settlers of the Big Sandy Valley were but slightly aware of the great mineral wealth which lay at their door. Although natural gas had been known from rock-fracture seepages such as that at Warfield on the Tug Fork, and at other points on the tributaries of the Levisa Fork, nothing was done about it. The immense deposits of natural gas which have been developed and indexed in Eastern

Kentucky were not even dreamed of by the pioneers. Petroleum became known through a number of seepages, but its quantity and value, and the many uses to which it might be put were wholly unknown. The existence of coal was practically unknown until about 1830,[17] and the vast quantities and excellent qualities of this fuel were, of course, never recognized during these early times. Salt was made from the several salt springs of the region, especially on the waters of Tug Fork near the Burning Spring, Paint Creek, Middle Creek and Beaver Creek. The Middle Creek springs, at which Daniel Boone wintered in 1767 and 1768, were well developed by 1795, and after 1800 supported a considerable local industry. There was a tradition through the land about the existence of silver and lead mines toward the headwaters of Paint Creek, which had been visited by one John Swift, it was said, as early as 1759. These mines, it was affirmed by Jennie Wiley and other returned captives, were known and had been used by the Indians from earliest times for the manufacture of lead bullets. But the early settlers of the Big Sandy were for the most part more concerned in proving up their new lands and hunting big game than they were in searching for these mythical deposits of metal. Over a century has passed, and the exact location of these far-famed Swift mines is still unknown and shrouded in mystery.

The Pioneer and His Times

In the year 1793 Edward Dobyns, Tax Commissioner of District No. 1 (Floyd County, then comprising the entire Big Sandy Valley and some adjacent territory) of Mason County, wrote just above his signature on the tax list:[18] "Coach and chariot wheels, other carriages with four wheels, carriages with two wheels, billiard tables and ferries, there is no such species of property within my district." Casually written in the probable fulfillment of his duties, this statement throws much light on the methods of transportation of the day. All journeys were made on horseback, a custom developed by necessity, which is still much in use in this region. As late as 1802 Judge John Graham brought from Mt. Sterling, Kentucky, on the backs of mules all of the wrought iron nails and window glass used in building his new home just below the mouth of Beaver Creek in the Big Sandy bottoms near the present village of Emma. This house was the first fine frame dwelling in the Big Sandy. It was

THE "GRAHAM CASTLE"

It was the first fine house in the "Valley." John Graham built it on his homestead tract in the broad bottom of the Levisa Fork below the "Mouth of Beaver." It was completed in 1807. By 1898 it had fallen into such disrepair that A. N. Leslie tore it down.

a story and a half high and had seven rooms. Five years were required for its construction.

While the new home was being built, Judge Graham lived with his family nearby in a low log house close to the bank of the river. Here he opened the first store or trading post of the region in 1800. He prospered and in 1815 began a genera. banking business. Loans ranging from $10.00 to $1,000.00 in American money were made from his personal funds. The notes always fell due on Christmas or New Year's day. Judge Graham was very precise in keeping his store and banking records. From his old home-made calf-bound account book, still existent and in the hands of his descendants in Prestonsburg,[11] are given below the names of most of the pioneers of that part of the Levisa River. The period covered is from 1800 to 1820, and the original spelling of the names has been retained.

A

Adams, Ben	Amyx, Joseph
Adams, William	Amyx, Peter
Adkins, Isom	Anderson, Micajah
Adkins, Spencer	Armstrong, George
Allen, Samuel	Arnold, ————
Allen, William	Auxer, Christopher
Allin, George	Auxer, Michael
Allin, Capt. Samuel	Auxer, Nathaniel
Allin, Samuel	Auxer, Thomas
Allin, William	Auxor, Simon

B

Baisden, John
Baisden, John L.
Banjay, George
Banjoy, George
Barnard, Valentine
Barnet, Jesse
Barnet, Nathaniel
Beavers, Capt. Abram
Beck, John
Belsher, George
Bench, Betsey
Berry, George
Bishop, George
Blantonship, William
Bloomer, Banjamin
Bowman, Elijah
Bradley, George
Branham, John
Brannum, David
Breading, John
Brown, Frances A.

Brown, George
Brown, James, Esq.
Brown, John
Brown, Robert
Brown, Robt., Jr.
Brown, Thomas
Brown, Thomas C.
Brumley, John
Bryant, James
Bunk, Christian
Bunks, Joanna
Bunton, Isaac
Burchet, Armsted
Burchet, Benjamin
Burchet, Drury
Burchet, John
Burchet, Sudduth Turner
Burchet, Thomas
Burchit, Benjamin
Burdin, Charles
Burgess, William

C

Cains, Richard
Calanry, James
Campbell, William
Cantirberry, ———
Cecil, Kensey B.
Chapman, I.
Childers, Pleasant
Christian, Thomas
Clark, Reuben
Click, John
Closser, Leonard
Cobourne, Edward
Cobourne, Samuel
Cockrell, William
Coins, Richard
Colier, Caiger
Colier, Meshac
Collier, Richard

Combs, Elizah
Combs, Mason
Combs, ———, Sr.
Conley, Henry
Conley, ———
Contra, Samuel Lain
Cooper, Robert
Cordell, William
Cox, William
Crabtree, Thomas
Craig, Robert
Crockett, John
Crum, Adam
Crum, Michael
Crumm, Henry
Cunning, James
Curnutt, John

D

Damron, John
Damron, Joseph
Damron, Lazarus
Damron, Moses
Damron, Moses, Jr.
Damron, Richard
Damron, Tazarus
Dartar, Nicholas
Darter, Henry
Darter, John

Davis, John
Davis, Lachariah
Dean, Job
Dean, John
DeLong, George
Delong, George
Denkins, James
Doris, Zachariah
Droddy, Ezekail
Dunbarr, Alexander

E

Eastep, Cornelius
Edwards, Merideth
Elkins, James
Elswick, Bradley
Elswick, Camond
Elswick, John, Sr.

Evans, John "Clutch"
Evans, John "Sandy"
Evans, Richard W.
Evans, Thomas
Ewing, Patrick

F

Ferguson, William
Fink, Daniel
Fitzpatrick, Jacob
Fitzpatrick, John
Ford, Isaac
Ford, Joseph

Foster, Isaac
Fraley, Isaac
Franklin, John
Frazer, Micajah
Fugate, Josiah

G

Gardner, Joseph
Garrit, Elimalick
Gent, Obediah
George, Jenny
Gerhart, Adam
Gerhart, Felty
Gibson, Archibold

Gilkey, Edward
Graham, William
Grant, Vincent
Griffith, David
Griffith, Robert
Grills, Capt. John

H

Hackworth, John
Hackworth, John
Haddix, John
Hager, John
Hager, George
Hail, Peter
Hall, William
Hambleton, David
Hambleton, Thomas
Hampton, Livingston
Handshew, Andrew
Hanna, Ebenezer
Hansley, Daniel
Hansley, James
Harins, John
Harman, Adam
Harmon, Adam
Harmon, Daniel
Harper, Stephen
Harris, David Kelsey
Harris, James
Harris, John

Harris, Nancy
Harris, William
Hatcher, John
Hatfield, Jeremiah
Hatfield, Martha
Hatfield, Sam
Haws, Jenny
Haws, John
Haws, Osral
Haws, Robert
Haws, Samuel
Haws, Samuel, Sr.
Hays, John
Hensley, George
Herral, Nathan
Herrall, William
Hickman, Isaac
Higgins, Capt. Robt.
Hogg, James
Holbrooks, Randoll
Horn, Frederick
Howes, Samuel

Jacobb, Walter
Jacobs, William
Jerome, Betsey
Johnes, Thomas
Johns, Thomas
Johnson, Barnabass
Johnson, John

Johnson, Thomas
Johnson, Zachariah
Jones, Isaac
Jones, Samuel
Justice, Johanan
Justice, Thomas

K

Karr, Samuel
Keaton, Barnet
Keaton, William
Kelly, Jesse Roberts
Kendrick, Patrick
Kesee, Richard

Kesner, Jacob
Kindrick, Patrick
King, Elisha
King, Isaac
Kitchen, Andrew

L

Lacey, James
Lacey, John C.
Lackey, Alexander
Lain, James L.
Larkin, Presley
Lee, Richard R.
Lewis, Benjamin
Lewis, Christopher
Lewis, Thomas

Little, William
Litton, Capt. Calob
Luster, William
Lycan, Hance
Lycan, James Gooding, Esq.
Lycan, Jerry
Lycan, John
Lycans, John

M

Mainer, Christopher
Manes, Jacob
Mankins, Walter
Mann, William
Mann, Samuel
Manore, Peter
Martin, David
Martin, George
Martin, William
Mathews, Reuben
Mault, Fanny
Mault, Moses
May, Daniel
May, Samuel
May, Thomas
Mayler, James
Mayo, Henry B.
Mayo, Johnathan
Mayo, Thomas
Mayo, Wm. James
Mayon, William I.
McAlester, Jean
McAlister, John
McBroom, Joseph
McBroom, William
McCallay, Thomas
McConnell, John M.
McConnil, John
McCoune, Isaac

McCoune, James
McCoune, John
McCoune, William
McCowell, John
McCoy, Samuel
McCoy, Walter
McCuyer, Solomon
McGuire, John
McGuyer, Cornelius
McGuyer, Squire
McGuyer, William
Mead, Abrel
Meed, Abral, Jr.
Meed, Jesse
Meed, Samuel
Menix, Charles
Millard, Abram
Millrons, Michael
Morgan, Col. David
Morgan, William
Morgans, Col. Hampton
Morris, Benjamin
Morris, Ezekail
Morris, John
Morris, Mrs. Mary
Morrison, Daniel
Morriss, Ben
Murphy, Zepahariah
Murry, Thomas

N

Nix, Elizabeth
Nix, Sally

Norman, Joseph

O

Osbourne, Sam
Osbourne, Thomas

Owens, Owen, Sr.
Owens, Thomas

P

Pack, Samuel
Patrick, Thomas
Patton, Christopher
Patton, Felix
Patton, Henry
Patton, James
Patton, James, Jr.
Patton, James, Sr.
Patton, John
Patton, Samuel
Patton, William G.
Perry, Arnal
Pierce, Benjamin
Pigg, James
Pinson, Aaron
Pinson, Allen

Pinson, Henry
Pinson, Jarrit
Pinson, John
Pinson, Thomas
Pinson, Thomas, Jr.
Pinson, William
Powell, Cader
Powell, Jacob
Power, Hollaway
Preece, Ruel
Preston, Moses
Preston, Nathan
Priest, John
Priest, Richard
Prince, William

R

Ratleiff, James
Ratleiff, Ruben
Ratleiff, Stephen
Ratleiff, William

Ratleiffe, Silus
Ratleiffs, Sarah W.
Ratlieff, Richard
Rice, Holeman

S

Sellards, John
Sellards, Samuel
Shoemaker, Jacob
Short, Samuel
Simmons, John
Sims, Martin
Sisson, Charles

Sisson, Emanuel
Skaggs, Charles
Sloan, George
Slusser, Jacob
Smiley, Samuel
Smith, Hardin
Smith, Harry

S—Continued

Smith, Joseph
Smith, William
Souders, Christian
Southerland, Alexander
Spears, Spencer
Spears, Thos.
Spurlock, Charles
Spurlock, John
Spurlock, Mathew
Spurlock, Nathan
Stafford, John
Stalcop, Peter

Starr, Coonrd
Stephens, Gilbert
Stratton, Harry
Stratton, Harry, Esq.
Stratton, Hiram
Stratton, James
Stratton, John
Stratton, Richard
Stratton, Solomon
Stratton, Tandy
Sutherland, Alexander

T

Tackett, John
Tackett, William
Terry, Miles
Thompson, John
Tolar, Christopher

Trimble, David
Triplett, Thomas
Turman, John
Turner, Suddith

V

Vaughn, Benjamin

W

Wallace, Timothey
Ward, James
Ward, James, Jr.
Ward, James, Sr.
Ward, John
Ward, Solomon
Weatherow, John
Webb, George
Webb, Wm.
Weddington, Henry
Wells, Wm.
Wiley, Thomas
Williams, Aldern

Williams, Hammon
Williams, John
Williams, Marion
Williams, Masson
Wilson, Harris
Wilson, James
Wilson, Robert
Wireman, John
Witten, Samuel
Witten, Thomas
Witten, Thomas, Sr.
Witten, William
Wyilei, Thomas

Y

Young, Alexander
Young, Charles W.
Young, James
Young, James, Esq.

Young, James, Jr.
Young, John
Young, Patrick
Young, Robt.

BIG SANDY ROADS

The early settlers of the Big Sandy Valley, traveling long distances by foot and horseback, principally over old Indian trails, gradually came to recognize the importance of establishing overland routes to the east and to the west. With the thought of placing themselves on a line of through traffic from the older settlements in Virginia to central Kentucky, there was outlined in the early part of the nineteenth century a transmontane route. This route came in over the gap of Levisa Fork, passed down the Big Sandy to the mouth of Paint Creek, and thence proceeded westward, crossing the Licking Valley through West Liberty and Hazel Green to Mt. Sterling and central Kentucky. Another route led from Mt. Sterling and Owingsville eastward through Grayson to Catlettsburg at the mouth of the Big Sandy, and thence on to the east, up the Ohio and Kanawha rivers.

The main or upper Big Sandy Road was connected by a route up Shelby Creek and Elkhorn to a road which came in from Richmond, following up the north fork of the Kentucky River, and led into the Pound River Valley through Pound Gap.[19] A great many

THE UPPER BIG SANDY

A characteristic old time view looking west up the Pound Fork from the home of John F. Skidham in Wise County, Virginia. Big Black Mountain is in the distant background. The best roads that the region afforded were found in broad bottoms of this type.

cattle were driven over these roads, which became well known to drovers and homesteaders who were on their way to the West. These roads were originally largely surveyed and constructed through Kentucky State funds, and thus portions of them frequently received the name of ''State Road,'' which has persisted to the present. They were, however, never really good roads. Poorly graded, subject to floods, without bridges, and undrained, these through routes of travel, early proposed as main highways, were later abandoned. Falling into county control they were not maintained, and finally became almost impassable.

Heroes and Home Folks

The Big Sandy Valley, long recognized as a favorite Indian hunting-ground, was won through many a bloody encounter by as valorous a group of Englishmen as ever lived. The original settlers of the Big Sandy carried their axes in one hand and their rifles in the other as they went about their work in the field and forest. The women, inured to danger and hardship, early learned the lessons of heroic self-confidence and woodcraft. Is it any wonder then that in the years which were to follow, when the nation's honor was at stake in 1812 and 1814, and again in the Mexican War of 1846 and 1847, that the Big Sandy gave with a prodigal hand of its sons to assist in the winning of these struggles so important in the life and continental expansion of the new nation? Young men from the backwoods of the Big Sandy were strapped to the rigging of Commodore Perry's ships off Put-in-Bay, Lake Erie, September 10, 1813, and did deadly work when turned upon the British seamen. Others marched with Governor Shelby and reinforced General Harrison. They made the great victory in Canada at the Battle of the Thames, October 5, 1813, possible and closed the campaign in the Northwest.[20] Men and boys from the Big Sandy were again with Andrew Jackson at New Orleans, leveling their trusty long-barreled squirrel rifles on the massed British regulars, and so won that great though needless victory for American arms. Trained from boyhood to the rifle and a sparing use of ammunition in their native hills, is it any wonder that they everywhere distinguished themselves for bravery and accuracy of fire, until it was said that "no bullet from the gun of a Kentucky mountaineer failed to find its mark"?

The middle of the nineteenth century closes the romantic period in the settlement of the

Big Sandy Valley. All the Indian questions had been settled. The age-old control of the British had been overthrown, and the country had been opened to a peaceful settlement and development through the perseverance and heroism of the hardy backwoodsmen. At this time the distant rumbling of fratricidal strife had not yet penetrated this beautiful, though remote, part of Kentucky. Railroads threading the quiet valley with a sad combination of material advancement and social pollution were yet unknown. Labyrinthine coal mines beneath the unnamed hills, and countless oil and gas wells piercing the earth to its very depths had never been proposed. In 1850 the Big Sandy Valley of Kentucky, filled with a pure and virile American blood, was a region of good though plain living, unusual hospitality, and delightful mountain charm.

NOTES TO CHAPTER VI

[1] See Appendix C. The Establishment of Floyd County, Kentucky.

[2] History of Kentucky. Collins. Vol. II, pp. 238-239.

[3] History of Kentucky. Kerr, Vol. I, p. 516.

[4] History of Kentucky. Collins. Vol. II, pp. 679-680.

[5] History of Kentucky. Collins. Vol. II, pp. 459-461.

[6] Big Sandy News. Vol. XXXVII, No. 52. Louisa, Kentucky.

[7] History of Kentucky. Collins. Vol. II, pp. 545-593. Also see Appendix B, The Division of Fincastle County and the Establishment of Mason County.

[8] Kentucky a Part of Virginia, Duke, in The South in the Building of a Nation. Vol. I, p. 248.

⁹ Tour, Cuming, in Early Western Travels. Thwaites. Vol. IV. Cuming's Tour, p. 154.

¹⁰ Tour, Cuming, in Early Western Travels. Thwaites. Vol. IV. Cuming's Tour, p. 154.

¹¹ Original Cash Book of John Graham, now in possession of Mrs. William Buck (Harris) Dingus, Prestonsburg, Ky.

¹² Letters from America, Flint, in Early Western Travels. Thwaites. Vol. IX. Flint's Letters, pp. 112-113.

¹³ A Visit to North America and the English Settlements in Illinois, Welby, in Early Western Travels. Thwaites. Vol. XII, p. 214. Also Vol. III.

¹⁴ The Big Sandy Valley. Ely, p. 20.

¹⁵ The Big Sandy Valley. Ely, p. 21.

¹⁶ History of Kentucky. Collins, Vol. II, p. 42.

¹⁷ The Big Sandy Valley. Ely, p. 21.

¹⁸ (Original) Tax List for District No. 1 (Floyd County) of Mason County, 1793. Archives Kentucky State Historical Society, Frankfort, Kentucky.

¹⁹ Kentucky Mountains. Verhoeff, pp. 133-160.

²⁰ The Battle of the Thames. B. H. Young.

APPENDIX

A

REVOLUTIONARY WAR SOLDIERS IN THE BIG SANDY VALLEY, KENTUCKY[1]

Floyd County, Kentucky

PENSIONERS UNDER THE ACT OF MARCH 18, 1818

Bouney, Joseph, private....................Virginia line
Caines, Richard, private....................Virginia line
Childres, Pleasant, private................N. Carolina line
Ferguson, William, private..............Pennsylvania line
Hopkins, Garner, private..................New York line
Haney, William, private....................Virginia line
Jones, Gabriel, private....................N. Carolina line
Jacobs, Roby, private......................Virginia line
Jones, Ambrose, private....................Virginia line
Murray, Thomas, private..............Pennsylvania line
Mullins, John, private.....................Virginia line
Preston, Nathan, private...................Virginia line
Preston, Moses, private....................Virginia line
Stone, Cudbeth, private...................Maryland line
Smith, 3rd, John, private..................Virginia line
Sullivan, Peter, private...................Virginia line
Young, Alexander, private................S. Carolina line

Pensioners Under the Act of June 7, 1832
(Began March 4, 1831)

Brown, Thomas C., cornet.................Virginia militia
Camron, James, private....................Virginia line
Connelly, Henry, captain of cavalry..North Carolina militia
Darten, Edward, private....................Virginia line
Fairchild, Abina, private.................N. Carolina line
Harris, James, private....................Virginia militia
Hitchcock, Joshua, private................N. Carolina line
Justice, Simeon, drummer................N. Carolina line
Moore, John, private.....................N. Carolina line
Pytts, Jonathan, private..................N. Carolina line
Patrick, James, private..................Virginia militia
Porter, James, private...................Virginia militia
Wadkins, Benedict, private..............N. Carolina line
Wells, Richard, private..................N. Carolina line

Pensioners in 1840[2]

Hall, Anthony
Pitts, Mexico
Thacker, Reuben
Williams, Philip
Henrel, Rebecca (widow)
Justice, Amy
Moore, Sally

Preston, Elizabeth
Harris, Patey
Porter, John
Brown, Elizabeth
Brown, Samuel
Regem, Samuel

Pike County

Dailey, Dennis, private. ....Virginia line
Adkinson, James, private....................Virginia line
Ford, Joseph, private....................N. Carolina line
Jackson, James, private.................N. Carolina line
Stipp, Moses, private....................S. Carolina line
Trant, Christian

Lawrence County

Atkinson, David, private....................Virginia line
Bates, William, private....................Virginia line
Burges, Edward, private....................Virginia line
Brown, William, private....................Virginia line
Blumer, Gilbert, private.................New York militia
Cox, William, private....................Virginia militia
Castle, Basil, private........................Virginia line
Crum, Adam, private....................N. Carolina line
Davis, Joseph, private....................Virginia line
Hardwick, George, private.................Virginia line

A BIG SANDY CEMETERY

This old burial ground is located at the mouth of Dry Creek on Right Beaver Creek in Floyd County. In the early days it was quite a common custom in the Sandy Valley to build wooden shelters over newly made graves. This view of the Hall cemetery was taken in the middle eighties.

Lyon, William, private................N. Carolina line
Lee, Samuel, private...............Virginia militia
Lastey, John, private................Virginia line
Marcum, Josiah, private...............Virginia militia
Marshal, John, private.................Virginia militia
Norton, James, private................Virginia militia
Pratt, James, private..................Virginia line
Perkins, George, private...............N. Carolina militia
Sexton, John, private.................S. Carolina militia
Ward, James, private......................Virginia line
Wooten, Silas P., private..................Virginia line

MEXICAN WAR VETERANS[3] WHO WERE RESIDENTS[4] OF THE BIG SANDY VALLEY, KENTUCKY

John W. Keller, enrolled 3rd Sergeant; mustered in April 12, 1847, at Prestonsburg; mustered out August 5, 1848, at Newport.

Robert Brown, enrolled private; mustered in April 12, 1847, at Prestonsburg; mustered out August 5, 1848, at Newport.

Charles Foster, enrolled private; mustered in April 28, 1847, at Louisa; mustered out August 5, 1848, at Newport.

Elihu Hawkins, enrolled private; mustered in April 15, 1847, at Prestonsburg; mustered out August 5, 1848, at Newport.

Thomas D. Hart, enrolled private; mustered in April 19, 1847, at Prestonsburg; mustered out August 5, 1848, at Newport.

W. J. Whitley, enrolled private; mustered in April 12, 1847, at Prestonsburg; mustered out August 5, 1848, at Newport.

John H. Brown, enrolled private; mustered in April 28, 1847, at Louisa; died July 26, 1848, near mouth of Salt River, in Ohio River.

B

THE DIVISION OF FINCASTLE COUNTY, AND THE ESTABLISHMENT OF MASON COUNTY, KENTUCKY

An act containing so much of every act or acts as ascertains the boundary of the State, and of the several counties.[5]

1776 State Boundary

Approved February 25, 1777. From and after the last day of December next ensuing, the said county of Fincastle shall be divided into three counties, that is to say, all that part thereof which lies to the south and westward of a line beginning on the Ohio, at the mouth of Great Sandy Creek, and running up the same and the main or northeasterly branch thereof to the Great Laurel Ridge, or Cumberland Mountain; thence southwesterly along the said mountain to the line of North Carolina, shall be one distinct county, and called and known by the name of Kentucky.

1788 Mason

From and after the first day of May next, the county of Bourbon shall be divided into two distinct counties, that is to say: All that part of the said county lying northeast of a line to begin at the junction of Licking with the Ohio; thence up the main creek of Licking to the head thereof; thence a direct line to strike the nearest part of Russell County line; thence along the said line to Big Sandy, and down the same to the Ohio; thence down the Ohio River to the beginning, shall be one distinct county, and called and known by the name of Mason; and the residue of the said county shall retain the name of Bourbon.

C

THE ESTABLISHMENT OF FLOYD COUNTY, KENTUCKY

An Act Forming a New County Out of the Counties of Fleming, Mason and Montgomery[6]

Section 1. Be it enacted by the General Assembly, that from and after the first day of June, 1800, all that part of the counties of Fleming, Montgomery and Mason, included in the following boundary, to-wit: Beginning at the mouth of Beaver Creek, near the narrows of Licking; thence north thirty degrees east to the Mason line; thence with said line to a point opposite the head of Little Sandy; thence a straight direction to the forks of Great Sandy; thence along the division line between this state and the state of Virginia to the head-waters of the main branch of Kentucky; thence down the same to the mouth of Quicksand; thence a straight line to the fifty-mile tree on the state road; thence along said road in a direction to Mount Sterling, to Blackwater; thence down the same to the mouth thereof; thence down Licking to the beginning, shall be one distinct county, and called and known by the name of Floyd. But the said county of Floyd shall not be entitled to a separate representation, until the number of free male inhabitants therein contained, above the age of twenty-one years, shall entitle them to one representative, agreeable to the ratio that shall hereafter be established by law.

Sec. 2. A court for the said county shall be held by the justices thereof, on the first Monday in every month, except the months in which the courts of quarter sessions are held, after the said division shall take place, in like manner as is provided by law in respect to other counties, and as shall be by their commissions directed.

Sec. 3. The justices to be named in the commission of the peace for the said county of Floyd, shall meet at the house of James Brown, in the said county, on the first court day after the said divisions shall take place, and having taken the oaths prescribed by law, and a sheriff being legally qualified to act, the justices shall immediately proceed to appoint and qualify a clerk, and fix on a place for holding courts in said county; then the court shall proceed to erect the public buildings in such place; and until such buildings are completed, shall appoint such place for holding courts as they may think proper, provided always, that the appointment of a clerk, and of a place for erecting the public buildings, shall not be made, unless a majority of the justices of the court of said county concur therein; but such appointment shall be postponed until some court day when a majority can be had; but the said court may appoint a clerk pro tempore. And it shall be lawful for the sheriffs of the counties of Fleming, Montgomery and Mason to collect and make distress for any public dues or officers' fees which shall remain unpaid by the inhabitants of the respective counties, at the time the division shall take place, and shall be accountable for the same in like manner as if this act had not been made, and the courts of the counties of Fleming, Montgomery and Mason shall have jurisdiction in all actions in law or equity that shall be depending before them at the time of the division; and shall try and determine the same, issue process, and award execution.

Sec. 4. The court of quarter sessions for the said county shall be held, annually, in the months of March, June, September and December, on the first Monday in each.

This act shall commence and be in force from and after the first day of June next.

Approved Dec. 13, 1799.

D

FIRST FLOYD COURT OF RECORD

NOTE—There is given herewith the earliest preserved record of court proceedings in the circuit and county of Floyd, which at the times included the entire Big Sandy Valley. This copy was made under the name of H. C. Stephens, Clerk of the Floyd Circuit Court, by W. C. Goble, D. C.

"At a Circuit Court held for the Circuit and County of Floyd at the house of William James Mayo in the town of Prestonsburg (the courthouse being lately destroyed by fire) on Monday the 18th. day of April 1808,

"Present The Honorable John Graham and Alexander Lackey Esqs. Assistant Judges.

"David Brown Gent. having made it appear to the satisfaction of the Court that he had obtained license to practice as an attorney at Law whereupon he qualified and took the oath prescribed by the act of the General Assembly in that case made and provided & hath leave to Practice in this Court.

"Abrham Beavers foreman, Jacob Slusher, Richard Priest, James Ratliff, Richard Ratliff, John Murphy, Richard Damron, Tandy Stratton, John Branham, John Hatcher, James P.

Harris, Harris Wilson, Alexander Young, Thomas Brown, James Young and Robert Brown, were sworn and empanneled a Grand Jury of inquest for the body of this Circuit, who after having received a charge from William P Fleming Gent. retired to consult on their presentments, and after some time returned into Court and having made no presentments were discharged.

"Ordered that this court adjourn until tomorrow morning 9 O'Clock.

"John Graham." (Judge)

Page 1 Completed Orders
Book—Floyd Circuit Court
1808-1818.

E

First Plan of Prestonsburg

Note—The following is an accurate copy of the official record relative to the location of the city of Prestonsburg. A photograph of this record is shown opposite page 150. As indicated below, this is a copy of the first record, which was lost when the first Floyd County Courthouse burned. The original spelling and punctuation have been retained. This survey was made originally on May 3, 1797, while the Big Sandy Valley was a part of Mason County. John Graham was at this time a Deputy Surveyor of Mason County, living near Prestons Station, which later became Prestonsburg:

Deed Book "A," Page 66.

Floyd County Records

A plan of a Town laid of on the north side Sandy River opposite the mouth of middle

Creek, and to be known by the name of Prestonsburg as surveyed May 3rd 1797, by direction of Mayor Andrew Hood, Matthias Harman and Solomon Stratton Agents for the adventurers on Sandy under Col John Prestons Grant. The Town is divided into two parts, the upper or that which lies above the branch consists Of 24 half acre lots, the lower part consists of 6 half acre lots the streets is 33 feet in width, running with 35° West along the river and the cross Streets North 55° East the lots are 444 poles in front and 18 poles in length. There is also surveyed adjoining s^d Town 30 five acre lots in peralelograms the same direction with the streets and are of the following Dimensions. No. 1, 2, 3, 4, 5 & 6 are 86.86 9.21 Poles No. 7, 8, 9, 10, and 11 are 72.36 by 11.05 poles No. 12, 13, 14 are 75 by 10.68 poles No. 15 is 100 by 8 poles No. 16 is 91 by 8.79 poles No. 17 is 82 by 9.75 poles No. 18 is 100 by 8 poles No. 19 is 88 by 9.49 poles No. 1 & 2 in lower Town is 52.20 by 15.32 poles No. 3, 4, 5, 6 is 60 by 13.32 poles, No. 7, 8, 9, 10, 11 is 40 by 20 poles, and there is 14 half acre lots on the River side of the main street And a Twenty Acre lot on the upper end of the Town.

                    John Graham, D.S.M.C.
Floyd County September Court 1810.

Ordered that the Clerk of this Court record this plat of the town of Prestonsburg in his

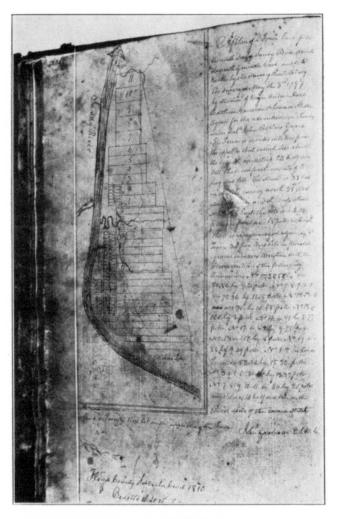

FIRST MAP OF PRESTONSBURG

This plat was made and described by John Graham who acted as Floyd County Surveyor in 1810. It may be found in Deed Book "A," page 66, of the Floyd County Clerk's records.

office again as the former records were burnt.
A Copy Rest: Wm. J. Mayo, C.F.C.C.

F

March Court 1822. 1st Day
STATE OF KENTUCKY
PIKE COUNTY to-wit:
(Pike County Court Commenced)

Be it remembered that at the house of
Spencer Adkins on Monday the fourth day of
March in the year of our Lord one thousand
Eight Hundred and Twenty Two, it being the
first Monday in said month of March Semeon
Justice, James Roberts, Rheuben Retherford,
John Hunt, and John Bevins produced Com-
missions from under the hands of John Adair
Governor of this Commonwealth of Kentucky
with the seal of the said Commonwealth
thereto affixed appointing them the said Semeon
Justice, James Roberts, Rheuben Retherford,
John Hunt, and John Bevins Justices of the
Peace in and for said County of Pike and
therefore the said Semeon Justice the first
numbered in said Commissions before the said
James Roberts the second numbered in said
Commissions did on the Holy Evanglist of
Almighty God took as well the oath to support
the Constitution of the United States and of
this State as the oath of Justice of the Peace
together with the oath prescribed by the act

of Assembly Entitled an act more effectually to surpress the practice of duelling and then the said Semeon Justice Administrated on the Holy Evangelist of Almighty God to the said James Roberts, Rheuben Retherford, John Bevins, and Hunt the persons in the said Commission as well to support the Constitution of the United States and of this State as the Oath of a Justice of the Peace together with the oath more effectually to surpress the practice of Dueling and thereupon a court was formed for the said County of Pike and now here at a Court held agreeable to the act of Assembly Establishing the County of Pike approved the nineteenth day of December one thousand Eight Hundred and Twenty one at the house of Spencer Adkins as aforesaid on Monday the fourth day of March (being the first Monday) therein *anidominia* one thousand Eight hundred and twenty two and in the thirtieth year of the Commonwealth of Kentuck.

Present Semeon Justice, James Roberts, Rheuben Retherford, John Hunt, and John Bevins, Esqs. Gentlemen Justices.

STATE OF KENTUCKY,
COUNTY OF PIKE..SCT.

I, W. A. May, Clerk of the County Court for the County and State aforesaid, certify that the foregoing is a true and correct copy of the

order of the First County Court Held in Pike
County on the fourth day of March, 1822, as
appears on record in Pike County Court Order
Book, Pages 1 and 2.

WITNESS my hand this 28th day of March,
1923.

W. A. MAY, Clerk.

By BESSIE RIDDLE, D. C.

NOTES ON APPENDIX

[1] Kentucky Pension List, 1812. Also A Census of Pensioners for Revolutionary or Military Services with their names, ages, and places of residence, as returned by the marshals of the several judicial districts under the act for the Sixth Census, 1841. Also Year Book of the Kentucky Society, 1896.

[2] History of Kentucky. Collins, Vol. I, p. 6.

[3] Taken from the Muster Roll of Company "E," 16th Regt. U. S. Infantry, Col. John W. Tibbatts, called into the service of the United States for the Mexican War, being one of the battalion of four companies organized in Kentucky, and officered by the President of the United States. Act of Congress, February 11, 1847, pp. 158-161 of Report of the Adjutant General of the State of Kentucky. Mexican War Veterans, pp. 158-160, Frankfort, 1889.

[4] Besides the seven soldiers named, there is good reason to believe there were other Big Sandians in the Mexican War. Due to the fact that their enlistment took place at points along the Ohio River, like Newport and elsewhere, it is impossible to trace them in the official records, either at Frankfort or Washington.

[5] Chap. CIII, Acts of the General Assembly of Kentucky, pp. 364, 365, 366, 367, 1797.

[6] Acts of Gen. Assembly of Ky., Chap. CXCI, pp. 282-283, 1799.

BIBLIOGRAPHY

Of the History of the Big Sandy Region
Prior to the Year 1850

(125 Titles)

Alvord, Clarence W., and Bidgood, Lee:
First Explorations of the Trans-Allegheny Region by the Virginians, 1650-1674. The Arthur H. Clark Co., Cleveland, 1912.

Arthur, T. S., and Carpenter, W. H.:
The History of Kentucky. Lippincott, Grambo & Co., Philadelphia, 1854.

Barker, Elihu:
Map of the State of Kentucky from Actual Survey. Philadelphia, 1795.

Beckwith, H. W.:
French Explorations, 1673-1682. *Illinois Historical Collections,* Vol. I. Springfield, 1903.

Brown, John Mason:
Memoranda of the Preston Family. S.I.M. Major, Frankfort, Ky., 1870.

Butler, Mann:
A History of the Commonwealth of Kentucky. Wilcox, Dickerman & Co., Louisville, 1834.

Butts, Charles:
Coal Resources and General Geology of the Pound Quadrangle of Virginia and Kentucky. U. S. Geological Survey Bulletin 541-F, 1914.

Cleveland, Catherine C.:
The Great Revival in the West—1797-1905. University of Chicago Press, 1916.

Collins, Lewis:
Historical Sketches of Kentucky. Lewis Collins (Pub.), Maysville, Kentucky, and S. A. and U. P. James, Cincinnati, 1850.

Collins, Richard H.:
History of Kentucky, 2 Vols. Collins & Co., Covington, 1882.

Colton, J. H.:
Map of Kentucky and Tennessee, 1856.
Map of the United States of America, etc. New York, 1847.

Connelley, William Elsey:
The Founding of Harman's Station. The Torch Press, New York, 1910.

Cotterill, R. S.:
The Old Maysville Road, in *Kentucky Magazine,* Vol. I, No. 6, December, 1917.
History of Pioneer Kentucky. Johnson & Hardin, Cincinnati, 1917.

Crandall, A. R.:

Coals of the Big Sandy Valley. Kentucky Geological Survey, Series III, Bulletin 4, 1905.

Preliminary Report on the Geology of Morgan, Johnson, Magoffin and Floyd Counties. Kentucky Geological Survey, Series II. No date.

Report on the Coal Beds of the Tug Fork Region, Martin and Pike Counties, Kentucky. Geological Survey, Series III. Report of Progress for 1908-09. Frankfort, 1910.

Croghan, George:

A Selection of George Croghan's Letters and Journals Relating to Tours into the Western Country, 1750-1765. Reprinted in Thwaites *Early Western Travels*, Vol. I.

Cuming, Fortescue:

A Tour to the Western Country, 1807-1809. Pittsburgh, 1810. Reprinted in Thwaites *Early Western Travels*, Vol. IV.

Davidson, Robert:

History of the Presbyterian Church in Kentucky. E. O. Jenkins, New York, 1847.

De Hass, Wills:
  History of the Early Settlement and Indian Wars of Western Virginia. H. Hoblitzell, Wheeling and Philadelphia, 1851.

Drake, Daniel:
  Pioneer Life in Kentucky. The Robert Clark & Co., Cincinnati, 1870.

Draper, Lyman C.:
  Manuscript 5 C 38: Personal letter from Richard Apperson, dated Mt. Sterling, Kentucky, May 29, 1854. Archives Wisconsin Historical Society, Madison.

Duke, Basil W.:
  Kentucky a Part of Virginia, 1606-1792, in *The South in the Building of the Nation,* Vol. I. Southern History Publishing Society, Richmond, Virginia, 1909.

Ely, William:
  The Big Sandy Valley. Central Methodist, Catlettsburg, 1887. (A book of 500 pages, devoted chiefly to biographies.)

Evans, Estwick:
  A Pedestrious Tour, 1818. Concord, New Hampshire, 1819. Reprinted in Thwaites *Early Western Travels,* Vol. VIII.

Evans, Lewis:

An Analysis of a General Map of the Middle British Colonies, in America, etc. Philadelphia, 1755. Map published according to act of Parliament, June 23, 1855.

Filson, John:

Map of Kentucky, 1784.

Flint, James:

Letters from America, 1818-1820. Edinburgh, 1822. Reprinted in Thwaites *Early Western Travels,* Vol. IX.

Floyd County:

Floyd County Records in Archives Floyd County Court House, Prestonsburg, Ky., 18.

Giles, Albert W.:

The Geology and Coal Resources of Dickenson County, Virginia. Virginia Geological Survey Bulletin No. XXI, 1921.

Graham, John:

Original Cash Book of John Graham of Prestonsburg, Kentucky. Graham Family Archives.

Green, Thomas Marshall:

The Spanish Conspiracy. The Robert Clark Company, Cincinnati, 1891.

Hale, John P.:

Trans-Allegheny Pioneers. Cincinnati, 1886.

Hall, James:
Pioneer Travels in Kentucky in *Legends of the West*. Philadelphia, 1832. Republished as Chapter IV, in Vol. XI of *Historic Highways of America*. The Arthur H. Clark Co., Cleveland, 1904.
Sketches of History, Life and Manners in the West, Vol. I. Harrison Hall, Philadelphia, 1835.

Harvey, Henry:
History of the Shawnee Indians, 1681 to 1854. Ephraim Morgan & Sons, Cincinnati, 1855.

Henderson, Archibald:
The Conquest of the Old Southwest. The Century Co., New York, 1920.

Hill, Sam E.:
(See Report of the Adjutant General of Kentucky, 1889, under Kentucky.)

Hoeing, Joseph Bernard:
Coals of the Upper Big Sandy Valley and the Headwaters of the North Fork of the Kentucky River, Kentucky. Geological Survey, Series IV, Vol. 1, Part I, 1913.
Oil and Gas Sands of Kentucky. Kentucky Geological Survey, Series III, Bulletin I, 1904.

Hulbert, Archer Butler:
Boone's Wilderness Road, Vol. VI of *Historic Highways of America.* The Arthur H. Clark Co., Cleveland, 1903. *The Ohio River—A Course of Empire.* G. P. Putnam's Sons, New York and London, 1906.

Huntington, Webster P.:
Kentucky and the Perry Victory Memorial, in *Kentucky Magazine*, Vol. I, No. 5, November, 1917.

Imlay, Gilbert:
Map of the State of Kentucky, 1793.
A Topographical Description of the Western Territory of North America. 3rd Edition. London, 1797.

Jillson, Willard Rouse:
First Explorations of Daniel Boone in Kentucky in *The Register of the Kentucky State Historical Society*, Vol. 20, No. 59, May, 1922. *Geologic Map of Kentucky*, 1920.
Oil and Gas Resources of Kentucky. Kentucky Geological Survey, Series V, Bulletin I, 1919.
Oil Field Stratigraphy of Kentucky. Kentucky Geological Survey, Series VI, Vol. III, 1922.

Jillson, Willard Rouse (Continued):

Paint Creek Pirate in *Economic Papers on Kentucky Geology*, Kentucky Geological Survey, Series VI, Vol. II. Paper No. XIII. Frankfort, 1921.

The Big Sandy Valley, in *The Register of the Kentucky State Historical Society*, Vol. 20, No. 60, September, 1922. Reprinted as A History of the Big Sandy Valley in the *Ashland Daily Independent*, Vol. XXVII, No. 243, pp. 1, 6 and 7, Sunday, October 15, 1922.

The Discovery of Kentucky, in *The Register of the Kentucky State Historical Society*, Vol. 20, No. 59, May, 1922.

The Migration of the Headwaters Divide of Right Middle Creek, Floyd County, Kentucky, in *Contributions to Kentucky Geology*, Kentucky Geological Survey, Series V, Bulletin IV, Paper No. VI. Frankfort, 1920.

Johnston, J. Stoddard:

First Explorations of Kentucky. Filson Club Publications, No. 13, Louisville, 1898.

Kentucky from 1792 to 1865, in *The South in the Building of the Nation*, Vol. I. Southern History Publishing Society, Richmond, Virginia, 1909.

Kentucky:

A Census of Pensioners for Revolutionary or Military Services. Blair and River, Washington, 1841.

Kentucky Pension Roll. A Statement, etc., of Floyd County, Kentucky. Bound, Printed Sheets, Archives Kentucky State Historical Society, Frankfort.

Kentucky Society Sons of the American Revolution. John P. Morton & Co., Louisville, 1896.

Laws of Kentucky. John Bradford, Lexington, 1799. Chapter CIII, Page 364, An Act approved February 25, 1797.

Records of the Land Office. New Capitol Frankfort, Kentucky.

The Register of the Kentucky State Historical Society. Twenty volumes, 1903-1922, Frankfort, Kentucky.

Report of the Adjutant General of the State of Kentucky. Mexican War Veterans. John D. Woods, Public Printer and Binder, Frankfort, 1889.

Tax List, Floyd County, 1793. Original Archives Kentucky State Historical Society, Frankfort.

Kerr, Charles:
History of Kentucky, 5 Vols. Judge Charles Kerr, editor, W. E. Connelley and E. M. Coulter, historical writers. American Historical Society, Chicago and New York, 1922.

Mather, W. W.:
Report on the Geological Reconnoissance Made in 1838. A Kentucky State Document, printed in Frankfort, 1839.

McAfee, Robert B.:
A History of the Late War in the Western Country. Worseley & Smith, Lexington, 1816.

M'Cullough, Samuel:
Map of Kentucky, showing the three original counties, Fayette, Jefferson and Lincoln. Original drawing in Archives Kentucky State Historical Society, 1835-1870.

Mease, James:
A Geological Account of the United States. Birch & Small, Philadelphia, 1807.

Michaux, Andre:
Travels into Kentucky, 1793-1796. Reprinted in Thwaites *Early Western Travels*, Vol. III.

Michaux, Francois Andre:
Travels to the West of the Allegheny Mountains, 1801-1803. London, 1805. Reprinted in Thwaites *Early Western Travels*, Vol. III.

Mitchell, S. Augustus:
Map of Kentucky and Tennessee, 1832.

Miller, A. M.:
Geology of Kentucky. Report of Geology and Forestry of Kentucky, Series V, Bulletin II, 1919.

Morrison, A. J.:
Travels in Virginia in Revolutionary Times. J. P. Bell & Co., Lynchburg, Virginia, 1922.

Munsell, Luke:
A Map of the State of Kentucky, also Parts of Indiana and Illinois, 1818.
(A Map of) *Kentucky* Reduced from Doct. Luke Munsell's large map of 1818, improved to the present time from authentic documents by the author. 1835.

Nuttall, Thomas:
Travels into the Arkansas Territory, 1819. Philadelphia, 1821. Reprinted in Thwaites *Early Western Travels*, Vol. XIII.

Ogden, George W.:
Letters from the West, 1821-1823. New Bedford, Mass., 1823. Reprinted in Thwaites *Early Western Travels*, Vol. XIX.

Ohio:
Ohio Archeological and Historical Society, Vol. I. Columbus, 1900.

Parkman, Francis:
LaSalle and the Discovery of the Great West. Third Part. Little, Brown & Co., Boston, 1907.

Pendleton, William C.:
History of Tazewell County and Southwest Virginia, 1748-1920. W. C. Hill Printing Co., Richmond, Virginia, 1920.

Phalen, W. C.:
Description of the Kenova Quadrangle. U. S. Geological Survey, Folio No. 184, 1912.
Economic Geology of the Kenova Quadrangle. U. S. Geological Survey Bulletin No. 349, 1908.

Pownall, Thomas:
A Map of the Middle British Colonies in North America. First published by Mr. Lewis Evans, in 1755; and since corrected, etc., published by J. Almon, London, 1776.

Redford, A. H.:

> *History of Methodism in Kentucky.* Southern Methodist Publishing House, Nashville, 1868.
> *Life and Times of H. H. Kavanaugh.* Nashville, 1884.

Ridpath, John Clark:

> *History of the United States.* Jones Brothers, Cincinnati, 1877.

Robertson, George:

> *Scrap Book on Law and Politics, Men and Times.* A. W. Elder, Lexington, 1855. (Archives, Kentucky State Historical Society.)

Schuchert, Charles:

> *Paleogeography of North America* in Bulletin of the Geological Society of America, Vol. 20, pp. 427-606, Pls. 46-101. February 5, 1910.

Semple, Ellen Churchill:

> *American History and Its Geographic Conditions.* Houghton Mifflin Co., New York and Boston, 1903.

Shaler, N. S.:

> *Kentucky, A Pioneer Commonwealth.* Houghton Mifflin Co., Boston and New York, 1884.

Smith, Z. F.:
History of Kentucky. Courier-Journal
Job Printing Co., Louisville, 1892.

Spalding, M. J.:
*Sketches of the Early Catholic Missions in
Kentucky,* 1787-1827. Louisville, 1844.

Sparks, Jared:
The Life of George Washington. Charles
Toppan, Boston, 1844.

Speed, Thomas:
The Wilderness Road. Filson Club Publications, No. 2, Louisville, 1886.

Spencer, J. H.:
A History of Kentucky Baptists. J. R.
Bams, Cincinnati, Ohio, 1885.

Spraker, Hazel Atterbury:
The Boone Family. The Tuttle Co., Rut-
land, Vermont, 1922.

Stone, Ralph W.:
*Coal Resources of the Russell Fork Basin
in Kentucky and Virginia.* U. S. Geological
Survey, Bulletin No. 348, 1908.
Elkhorn Coal Field, Kentucky. U. S.
Geological Survey, Bulletin No. 316, 1907.

Summers, Lewis Preston:
History of Southwest Virginia, 1746-1786. J. L. Hill Printing Co., Richmond, Virginia, 1903.

Thwaites, R. G.:
Early Western Travels, 1748-1846. A Series of Annotated Reprints in 32 Volumes. The Arthur H. Clark Co., Cleveland, 1904-07:

Vol. I. Croghan's *Tours into the Western Country.*

Vol. III. Andre Michaux's *Travels.*

Vol. III. F. A. Michaux's *Travels.*

Vol. IV. Cuming's *Sketches of a Tour.*

Vol. VIII. Evans' *Pedestrious Tour.*

Vol. IX. Flint's *Letters from America.*

Vol. XII. Welby's *Visit to North America.*

Vol. XIII. Nuttall's *Travels.*

Vol. XIX. Ogden's *Letters.*

On the Storied Ohio. A. C. McClurg & Co., Chicago, 1903.

Revolution on the Upper Ohio, 1775-1777. Wisconsin Historical Society, Madison, 1908.

Thwaites, Reuben Gold, and Kellogg, Louise Phelps:
Documentary History of Dunmore's War, 1774. Wisconsin Historical Society, Madison, 1905.

Venable, W. H.:
Beginnings of Literary Culture in the Ohio Valley. Robert Clark & Co., Cincinnati, 1891.

Verhoeff, Mary:
The Kentucky Mountains. Filson Club Publications No. 26, Louisville, 1911.
The Kentucky River Navigation. Filson Club Publications No. 28. Louisville, 1917.

Welby, Adlard:
A Visit to North America and the English Settlements in Illinois, 1819-1820. London, 1821. Reprinted in Thwaites *Early Western Travels,* Vol. XII.

Wentworth, Chester K.:
Russell Fork Fault of Southwest Virginia. Journal of Geology, Vol. XXIX, No. 4, pp. 351-369, May-June, 1921, and also *Russell Fork Fault* in Virginia Geological Survey, Bulletin No. XXI, pp. 53-67, Charlottesville, 1921.

West Virginia:
> *First Report, Department of Archives and History of West Virginia.* V. A. Lewis, Charleston, 1906.

Withers, Alexander Scott:
> *Chronicles of Border Warfare.* Edited by Thwaites, R. G., and Draper, L. C. The Robert Clark Company, Cincinnati, 1895.

Young, Bennett H.:
> *The Battle of the Thames.* Filson Club Publications, No. 18, Louisville, 1903.

The End

INDEX

A

Page

B